BADGER BRAIN TWISTERS

Wisconsin Trivia, Games, Puzzles, and More!

by Kelly Whitt

Trails Books
Madison, Wisconsin

Library of Congress Control Number: 2007936919
ISBN: 978-1-931599-97-9

Editor: Mark J. Knickelbine
Designer: Mark Porter

Printed in the United States of America.
12 11 10 09 08 07   6 5 4 3 2 1

Trails Books, a division of Big Earth Publishing
923 Williamson Street • Madison, WI 53703
(800) 228-5830 • www.trailsbooks.com

CONTENTS

Introduction

1

On the Map

5

Sports & Recreation

31

The Great Outdoors

55

History & Government

81

Food, Fame, & Fun

109

Answers

135

INTRODUCTION

Wisconsin is an eclectic state. From the forested playgrounds in the north to the rolling farmlands in south and central Wisconsin to the corridors of industry, business, and government in the Fox Valley, Milwaukee, and Madison metropolises, the state's people and activities are as diverse as the landscape.

But something Wisconsinites have in common is that they are a well-educated and proud lot. They are knowledgeable about their state and are happy to share that knowledge with others. They are also eager to discover new and fascinating facts about the place they call home.

Wisconsinites also know how to have fun. Sports provide exercise and entertainment in every season. Packer Backers revel in their team's small town roots and record championship titles; Badgers Fans, whether alumni or not, pack the stands for the dozen-plus sports in the athletic program; and Wisconsinites invent their own zany activities from the sausage races at Miller Park to ice bowling on frozen lakes.

Recreation in Wisconsin often involves communing with nature. There are more than 50 state parks and forests in Wisconsin plus recreation and natural areas, providing multiple opportunities for hunting, fishing, hiking, biking, camping, and more.

Mother Nature plays a big hand in the day-to-day life in our state. The tourism industry depends on weather ranging from warm sunny days in summer to piles of snow in winter. Tornadoes and ice storms have ripped apart communities, and farmers' livelihoods depend on good growing seasons.

Wisconsin's history is tied to the people who worked this land, first by hunting for furs, then through the timber industry, and now with farming. Our history is also a tale of explorers and Native Americans, the establishment of a government and the emergence of ghost stories anchored in our tumultuous past.

Test your knowledge of the Badger State with the puzzles and trivia in this book. Can you name the largest lake in Wisconsin? Where in Wisconsin was the nation's worst forest fire? What type of Native American-made landmarks dot the state? Which city is nicknamed "Little Switzerland"? Which actors from Wisconsin have made the big time? Can you name all the cities in Wisconsin that claim to be the UFO Capital of the World? The answers to these and much, much more are all inside.

To start you off in the right frame of mind, try this little brainteaser. If you take away all the letters that appear more than once in the word WISCONSIN and rearrange the remaining letters, what appropriate word is revealed?

Have fun, and… On, Wisconsin!

— Kelly Whitt

ON THE MAP

S H O T

O L A T A L

L F I

W C O N

O N U

A I L J E

K E Y S O

E R P E N

G L A D E

F A I R T R

Wisconsin's 34.8 million acres make it the twenty-third largest state and our population of five and a half million makes us the twentieth most populous. Most Wisconsinites now live in urban areas, although small-town traditions and country life are still an important part of our culture.

Wisconsin is carved into 72 counties. The first counties came into existence even before Wisconsin attained statehood in 1848. Wisconsin's earliest cities were located along major waterways. The names given to counties and cities are reflective of the people who were important to the area. Indian tribe names such as Outagamie, Winnebago, and Sauk, and Indian words such as Kewaunee ("river of the lost") and Sheboygan ("great noise underground") are now tied to the land. Early Wisconsin politicians and American presidents are represented in places named Douglas, Vilas, Dodge, Jackson, Monroe, and Madison, among others.

Thickly scattered on the Wisconsin map are the blue jewels of our state. Ancient glaciers made pockmarks in the land and left behind our plentiful lakes. Because glaciers bypassed the southwest portion of Wisconsin, few natural lakes lie within this region. Overall, Wisconsin is home to more than 15,000 lakes.

Wisconsin County Names

(crossword grid)

Across

1 In ___ and starts
5 Hit the mall
9 Fall behind
12 History
13 Glistened
14 New money in the Old World
15 Truant (abbr.)
16 Eagle claw
17 Nevada's ___ 51
18 Wisconsin county originally known as La Pointe County
20 Peak
21 Beloit to Hartford direction
22 Tiff
24 Wisconsin county named for Native American word for "plentiful with fish"
28 Wisconsin county named for Native American word for "good earth"
32 Thrash
33 "County" in England
34 Unit of weight for wool
35 Imitation
36 Parisian river
37 Kind of wrestler
38 Exist
39 Used up
40 Boss
41 Wisconsin county originally known as New County

43 Wisconsin county originally known as Bad Axe County
44 Breezy
45 Government spy group (abbr.)
46 Holler
49 Wisconsin county named after Ms. Julst, first white woman to settle in the area
54 Suspended
55 Pinkish hue
57 Shakespearean king
58 Fashion magazine
59 Scavenging animal in Africa
60 Asian garment
61 Call it a ___
62 Designer Cassini
63 Gaelic

Down

1 Target of exercise
2 Wisconsin neighbor
3 Helen of ___
4 Ego
5 Sedimentary rock
6 Capture
7 Yoko ___
8 Sty
9 Entice
10 Mars' Greek counterpart
11 Gouda's animal source
13 Office employee

14 Planet between Venus and Mars
19 Of other countries (abbr.)
20 Detective's job
22 Jude or Elmo, for example
23 Clean
24 Viscera
25 Ms. Barton
26 Made of a certain tree
27 Never (Ger.)
28 Complain
29 Take ___ for the worse (2 wds.)
30 Leading man
31 Decorate
33 Sordid
36 Box
37 Polite address
39 Thin opening
40 Listen
42 Measuring device
43 Bowed stringed instrument
45 Bell sound
46 Backyard structure
47 Hawaiian dance
48 My one and ___
49 Liberated
50 Nothing ___ matters
51 Close by
52 Autos
53 Great Lake
55 Comedienne Margaret
56 Olive ___, Popeye's girl

Solution on page 135.

Across

1 Wisconsin native fauna
5 Sensitivity
9 ___ black
14 Butter alternative
15 Abreast
16 Cognizant
17 Wisconsin's most populous county
19 Wanderer
20 City targeted in World War II
21 Shucks
23 ___ Latin
24 Lice
27 County that is Wisconsin's leading producer of potatoes, snap beans and carrots
29 Wisconsin's largest county
33 Caustic substance
34 Generation
35 Actor Quinn
37 Skim
41 Sour fruit
43 Taste appreciatively
45 Filled tortilla dish
46 Lights out signal
47 Wisconsinite and baseball head
49 Answer to Virginia?
50 Cobra

53 Wisconsin county with the slogan "Scenic bluffs and great river roads"
55 Wisconsin's smallest county
59 Periodic table member
60 Border
61 Puncturers
63 Artificial fat substance
67 Influence
69 Wisconsin's newest county
72 Sharp
73 Type of jacket or collar
74 Midday
75 Tear
76 Customary practice
77 Serf

Down

1 Capitol feature
2 Yalies
3 Congers
4 Ivanhoe's love
5 19th Greek letter
6 Ten Commandments vessel
7 Alverno student
8 Annoying person
9 Kitchen closet
10 ___ Jima
11 Busch Gardens location
12 An Internet list owner
13 Shrubbery row

18 Singer Baker
22 An Internet service provider
25 "With ___ ring…"
26 Pops
28 Quiz
29 Word after patty
30 Solo
31 Incline
32 Belly button
36 Pitcher Ryan
38 Islands
39 Pros
40 Front of an airplane
42 Brother with a bad deal
44 Lake in Wisconsin
48 Speaker of 25 Down
51 Maneuvered on the ice
52 Church row
54 Over a computer's modem
55 Whales
56 Nothing
57 Affair
58 Fudd's first name
62 Scientific project to contact aliens (abbr.)
64 Baseball player Slaughter
65 ___ Flux
66 Hawaiian bird
68 Shoshonean
70 Forget-me-___
71 ___ way or another

Solution on page 135.

7

Complete the puzzle by filling in all 72 names
of Wisconsin's counties.

Solution on page 136.

4 Letters
DANE
DOOR
DUNN
IOWA
IRON
POLK
ROCK
RUSK
SAUK
WOOD

5 Letters
ADAMS
BROWN
CLARK
DODGE
GRANT
GREEN
PEPIN
PRICE
VILAS

6 Letters
BARRON
FOREST
JUNEAU
MONROE
OCONTO
ONEIDA

PIERCE
RACINE
SAWYER
TAYLOR
VERNON

7 Letters
ASHLAND
BUFFALO
BURNETT
CALUMET
DOUGLAS
JACKSON
KENOSHA
LINCOLN
OZAUKEE
PORTAGE
SHAWANO
ST. CROIX
WAUPACA

8 Letters
BAYFIELD
CHIPPEWA
COLUMBIA
CRAWFORD
FLORENCE
KEWAUNEE
LA CROSSE
LANGLADE

MARATHON
RICHLAND
WALWORTH
WASHBURN
WAUKESHA
WAUSHARA

9 Letters
EAU CLAIRE
FOND DU LAC
GREEN LAKE
JEFFERSON
LAFAYETTE
MANITOWOC
MARINETTE
MARQUETTE
MENOMINEE
MILWAUKEE
OUTAGAMIE
SHEBOYGAN
WINNEBAGO

10 Letters
WASHINGTON

11 Letters
TREMPEALEAU

Read the 26 clues that follow. When you have figured out which county the clue is referring to, fill its name into the corresponding numbered blank. When complete, you will have 26 counties from A to Z.

1		A						
2		B						
3		C						
4		D						
5		E						
6		F						
7		G						
8		H						
9		I						
10		J						
11		K						
12		L						
13		M						
14		N						
15		O						
16		P						
17		Q						
18		R						
19		S						
20		T						
21		U						
22		V						
23		W						
24		X						
25		Y						
26		Z						

1 County home to High Cliff State Park
2 County that shares a name with Wisconsin's largest lake
3 County with Black River State Forest and named after 7th US President Andrew
4 County home to Horicon Marsh and named after a territorial governor
5 North woods recreational county named after an Indian tribe
6 County named for a formerly abundant plains animal
7 County in which Harry Houdini grew up
8 County home to Copper Falls State Park and bordering Lake Superior
9 County home to Burlington's Chocolate Fest and bordering Lake Michigan
10 County home to Necedah National Fish and Wildlife Refuge
11 County home to Devil's Lake State Park and Circus World Museum
12 County Frank Lloyd Wright was born in
13 The newest county; it consists entirely of an Indian reservation
14 The only county to border Door County
15 County named after the 5th US President James
16 County whose name means "mountain rising from waters"
17 County named for an early explorer in Wisconsin
18 County on the Minnesota border where an F3 tornado struck Siren in 2001
19 County named for the first US President
20 County home to the Wisconsin Maritime Museum
21 County named after Wisconsin's 13th governor; a University of Wisconsin observatory is also named for him
22 County with the most lakes and the town of Land O'Lakes
23 County home to Blue Mound State Park and the House on the Rock
24 County home to many Twin Cities workers
25 County home to the American Club
26 Smallest county; it's just north of Milwaukee

The 10 counties below are listed in alphabetical order. Read the descriptions that follow and try to match them to the Wisconsin counties they describe.

Bayfield County	**Juneau County**
Burnett County	**Lafayette County**
Calumet County	**Langlade County**
Fond du Lac County	**Richland County**
Iron County	**Sauk County**

1 With Hurley as its seat, this county is the least dense in the state with only nine people per square mile. The population here has declined since the early 1900s. Waterfalls, including two at a height of 90 feet, are some of this county's jewels. Its northern border abuts both Lake Superior and the Upper Peninsula of Michigan. Portions of the Bad River and Lac du Flambeau Indian Reservations and Chequamegon-Nicolet National Forest reside within its borders.

2 In 1897, 9,000-year-old mastodon bones were found in this county. Its southern edge sits on the Wisconsin River. Popp's Cave and Wisconsin's largest onyx cave, Eagle Cave, are found within its borders. As the birthplace of Frank Lloyd Wright, the county has turned a warehouse he designed into a museum honoring him. The county seat was a "dry" town, meaning that it did not allow sales of alcohol, until 1987. The town of Cazenovia made headlines in 2006 due to a deadly school shooting; the school sits on the border of Sauk County and this county.

3 This county's name means "bottom of the lake," appropriate for land that lies at the southern end of Lake Winnebago. Here you can find the Taycheedah Correctional Institution, where Lawrencia (Bambi) Bembenek was once a famous inmate and made her much-publicized escape. The community of Ripon is found in this county, which is the birthplace of Rippin' Good Cookies and the Republican Party. Ripon College is also here; Harrison Ford is its famous former student. Alliant Energy's wind-farm project is proposed for this county, and a devastating F5 tornado struck the town of Oakfield here in 1996.

4 Despite a military firing range, military reservation, and an interstate that cuts through it, this county is a haven for nature. The second largest lake in Wisconsin, Petenwell Lake, and the fourth largest, Castle Rock Lake, lie along its eastern border, fed by the Wisconsin River. The Central Wisconsin Conservation Area, Necedah National Fish and Wildlife Refuge, and Buckhorn State Park are also found here. The county was named for the man who founded Milwaukee and was the first mayor there. A shrine to the Virgin Mary was constructed in a spot here where a controversial apparition is said to have occurred more than 50 years ago.

5 This county was more active in the early days of our state; it was the center of the lead-mining boom and home to Wisconsin's first capitol at Belmont. The county has the only courthouse in the nation still in use whose construction was paid for by one man. It is a beautiful and imposing structure that cost $136,556.17 to build in 1907. The Cheese Country Trail runs through this county, and two state parks, Belmont Mound and Yellowstone Lake, can also be found here.

6 This county was home to two authors, August Derleth and Aldo Leopold. In 1867, it was briefly the center of hops production, growing one-fifth of the nation's total. The farmers here followed the short-lived and lucrative crazes at the time, soon producing sugar beets, flax, hemp, and finally dairy, which is still predominant today. In the mid-twentieth century, the Badger Army Ammunition Plant was a buzzing facility, supplying our troops in the Korean and Vietnam Wars. Devil's Lake State Park, the Circus World Museum, and Wisconsin Dells can all be found here.

7 Antigo is the county seat in this county, which was formerly known as New County. A winter playground, there are 11 snowmobile clubs that maintain 530 miles of trails. In summer, its 841 lakes provide various boating, fishing, and other water opportunities. The first county forest in Wisconsin was created here. The county is named after a French pioneer who fought for the Americans in the Revolutionary War.

8 Named after a French word for "peace pipe," this county is one of the wealthiest and fastest growing areas in the state. Situated on the east shore of Lake Winnebago, it is close to the Fox Valley, Green Bay, and Door County. Wisconsin's largest fossil collection resides in Ledge View Nature Center at Chilton, its county seat. Natural areas include High Cliff State Park and the Brillion Marsh. Effigy mounds can also be found in the area.

9 Large tracts of land are preserved in this county. The Glacial Lake Wildlife Complex is made up of Crex Meadows, Amsterdam Sloughs, Fish Lake, Danbury, and Namekagon Barrens Wildlife Areas. The Gandy Dancer Trail, situated on an abandoned Soo Line rail bed, runs through the county. One of the least developed river systems in the Midwest is preserved here in the St. Croix National Scenic Riverway. Hole in the Wall Casino and Hotel, Little Turtle Hertel Express Casino, and Sand Lake Bingo all reside within this county.

10 As the northernmost Wisconsin county, this is the gateway to the Apostle Islands. Its shoreline along Lake Superior hosts the largest fleet of chartered and rented sailing vessels in the nation. The county's point houses the Red Cliff Indian Reservation. It has the most conservation and recreation lands in the state, at 467,582 acres. Skiing is popular here; the county is the site of the annual Birkebeiner cross-country race and the Mount Ashwabay and Mount Telemark downhill ski areas.

Solution on page 136.

Wisconsin City Nicknames

Across

1 Mop
5 Octagonal sign
9 Pushpin
13 Home to Machu Picchu
14 Oscar winner O'Neal
16 Cross letters
17 Always
18 Bonus
19 School founded by King Henry VI
20 Casino employee
22 "Fun City, USA"
24 Aqueduct of Sylvius
26 Cheer
27 President James and Elizabeth
30 Berate
35 Police rank (slang)
36 ___ Alto, CA
38 Jason's ship
39 Bum
40 Fan
41 Hindu princess
42 Ratio words
43 Article
44 Fall flower
45 From there
47 In an unspecified way
49 ___ Not Unusual
51 Football maker

52 "Clown Town, USA"
56 Agitated
60 So be it
61 Actress Zellweger
64 Money of Italy
65 Chomp
66 Tugs
67 Den
68 Store
69 Bug spray ingredient
70 Dip a donut

Down

1 Raced
2 "Houston, ___ got a problem"
3 Zone
4 "Chocolate City, USA"
5 Audio system
6 Word after flat or income
7 Baseball player Mel
8 Cleaner
9 Level
10 Against
11 Gator's cousin
12 Knot
15 Bullfighter
21 To be (Fr.)
23 Alexander ___ Great
25 Transfer a plant
27 Bog

28 Give a speech
29 Fills
31 "Cheese City, USA"
32 Poetic muse
33 Nixon's VP
34 Café ___
35 Grilling skewer
37 Junky car
40 Type of supplement
44 Aviation prefix
46 104
48 Least
50 Golfer Sam
52 Blots
53 Send out
54 Mother of Apollo
55 Once again
57 Island party
58 ___ Brockovich
59 Dweeb
62 Janesville to Fond du Lac direction (abbr.)
63 Squeeze out

Solution on page 135.

All the words below are names of cities in Wisconsin. The words are encrypted in the same code. Can you break the code to read the names of all the cities? As a solving aid, the words are listed in alphabetical order. For an extra hint, see the bottom of the page.

1 VXQTX EWZVS

2 VMCYVJQSHTH

3 QSVESX FVU

4 QAVHICVXFEWAAS

5 QTMITQSA

6 IVUKQSAAMKTXZ

7 IXWEWZR

8 FSAVEVH

9 SLL CVXQTX

10 LSXUVHZTYH

11 CVRSA LXSSH

12 PVJPVJHV

13 AVHF T'AVPSM

14 UVKAS QAJOO

15 TITHTUTYTI

16 KVXFSSEWAAS

17 XWIS AVPS

18 MCVYVHT

19 YVJKVIV

20 YWMITHMWH XVKWFM

Hint: Number thirteen shares its name with a butter company.

Wisconsin City Code Names

Across

1 Fundamentals
5 Sand and silt
10 *A Farewell to* ___
14 Chicken hut
15 Decree
16 Boyfriend
17 *Vogue* rival
18 Colorful tropical fish
19 *The Dukes of Hazzard* Deputy
20 Prevent
22 Toni Morrison novel
24 Word after Victorian or Disco
25 *Star Trek* character
28 Code Name: Hairless succeed
30 Code Name: Red Planet corridor
34 Lake Wisconsin fish
35 *Bewitched* director Lupino
36 Reprimand
38 Beauty shop
42 Type of paper
44 Butler's torment
46 Actor Benicio Del ___
47 Kids
49 Accumulate
51 Big Ten school
52 Health club
54 Code Name: Fruit mother lode
56 Code Name: Deer scent self

60 Oldest son of Isaac
61 Spring Green Shakespearean group
62 Refute
64 Word before rib or number
68 Gush
70 Sister's daughter
73 Eternally
74 Mail
75 Recipient
76 Sharp
77 Greek god of love
78 Photographer Adams
79 Questions

Down

1 Scored a hole-in-one
2 Tree part used for lumber
3 Pony
4 Races
5 Allow
6 Single
7 Devours
8 Brush clean
9 German prisoner of war camp
10 Actor Vigoda
11 Freshen
12 Some New Zealanders
13 ___ G. Komen Breast Cancer Foundation

21 Cheers
23 Unfortunately
26 Mexican food staple
27 Hello and goodbye
29 Shucks
30 Light spray
31 *Queen for* ___ (2 wds.)
32 Level
33 Spitting animal
37 Hang loosely
39 Pillage
40 About (2 wds.)
41 Person, place, or thing
43 Office furniture
45 Egyptian snakes
48 Hied
50 Smack
53 Schedule
55 Ah ha!
56 En ___
57 Michigan's ___ Peninsula
58 Office worker
59 *The* ___ (farcical news source)
63 Desires
65 Actor Burl ___
66 Tame
67 European sea birds
69 ___ per min = wpm
71 Shoe width
72 Slippery swimmer

Solution on page 135.

The Wisconsin cities below are missing one letter. Can you recognize the cities and supply their missing letters? All the letters from A to Z will be used once, no letter is repeated.

1 AL__OMA

2 I__ONIA

3 BE__OIT

4 CA__LE

5 WAU__UN

6 PO__NETTE

7 ME__FORD

8 CEDARB__RG

9 CHENE__UA

10 CR__NDON

11 TO__AH

12 GRA__TON

13 SHA__ANO

14 OC__NTO

15 LAN__ASTER

16 MO__INEE

17 SPOO__ER

18 EP__RAIM

19 MA__INETTE

20 WAB__NO

21 MIL__ON

22 LOM__RA

23 STURTE__ANT

24 NE__OOSA

25 WAU__EKA

26 __UDA

The 10 cities below are listed in alphabetical order. Read the descriptions that follow and try to match them to the Wisconsin city each describes.

Hudson	**Sheboygan**
Kenosha	**Sparta**
New Glarus	**Stevens Point**
Oshkosh	**Sun Prairie**
Phillips	**Superior**

1 This city, sometimes referred to as the Gateway to Wisconsin, is the International Headquarters of the Barbershop Harmony Society. The famous film director, Orson Welles, hailed from here. Electric streetcars are a unique form of transportation in this city. A public museum and military museum reside here, as well as Jockey International's corporate headquarters. In the summer, the Bristol Renaissance Faire entertains visitors and takes them back in time. The community is popular among families who must commute to Milwaukee and Chicago.

2 This town in southcentral Wisconsin has earned the nickname "Little Switzerland." The Heidi Festival and Wilhelm Tell Festival are both held here. Settled by Swiss pioneers, the area has many structures built in the chalet-style of architecture. A wooded state park is just outside the city limits, and the 23-mile-long Sugar River Bike Trail begins in town. A brewing company of the same name resides here and produces many popular beers, including Spotted Cow and Uff-da Bock.

3 In 2004, this city was named the fourth best city in America in which to find rich, single men. The John Michael Kohler Arts Center, Kohler-Andrae State Park, and Maywood Environmental Park all call this city home. Known as the "Bratwurst Capital of the World," a summer festival called Brat Days is held here, which includes an eating contest that is aired on ESPN. Not surprisingly, the Johnsonville Sausage Company calls this city home. Sitting on Lake Michigan, shoreline cruises are available and the Blue Harbor Resort hosts conferences and water park fans alike.

4 The most famous person to come from this city is the artist Georgia O'Keefe. Its next famous resident is probably Jimmy the Groundhog, who makes his prediction for spring every February 2. NASCAR truck racer Todd Kluever also hails from here. The town holds an annual sweet corn festival in August. This forward-thinking community was one of the first in Wisconsin to become "wireless." A couple of odd laws are on the books here, including the rule that one may not ride a bicycle with one's hands off the handlebars.

5 A fire that burned 100,000 acres and much of the downtown almost wiped this city off the map in 1894. The Wisconsin Concrete Park here features more than 200 figures sculpted by Fred Smith. Just north of the highest point in the state, its slogan is "The Northwoods is our Backyard." In Sokol Park a unique monument stands in memory of Lidice, a Czech village razed to the ground after the Nazis exterminated its population.

6 The US Curling Association is headquartered in this city. Kathy Kinney, who played Mimi on *The Drew Carey Show*, hails from here. Sentryworld, a flower-filled, Robert Trent Jones Jr.-designed golf course, lies on the north side of town. Its nickname is "Gateway to the Pineries" and it is located near the center of the state on the Wisconsin River. A four-year college and well-known brewery are found here, and many tales of ghostly hauntings concern area cemeteries and bridges.

7 This city was popular with President Calvin Coolidge. He spent the summer of 1928 vacationing here and used the Central High School as his summer White House. The Whaleback Maritime Museum is here and this was the ill-fated *Edmund Fitzgerald's* last port. Take a boat trip of your own with Vista Fleet Harbor Cruises or take to the skies at Richard I. Bong Airport. Bikers can ride the Tri-County Corridor Trail from here to Ashland. The Fairlawn Mansion and Museum is open to visitors and Barker's Island is a center of recreation with its beaches, boat landing, and mini golf.

8 One end of the first rails-to-trails bike path in the state is located in this community found east of La Crosse and west of Fort McCoy. The "Bicycling Capital of America" has a giant statue of an old-fashioned biker known as Big Ben. Tourists also come for the Deke Slayton Space and Bike Museum and to browse arts and crafts made by the state's largest Amish community. FAST Corporation makes giant fiberglass objects, many of which can be seen on display on its property.

9 This city is best known for its fly-in celebration known as EAA AirVenture. A line of overalls began here in 1895; the company later made children's clothing. Located on the western shore of Lake Winnebago, the city is home to the Paine Art Center and Gardens and the Menominee Park and Zoo. Once the second largest city in the state, remnants of its affluent days survive, including the Grand Opera House.

10 One of the fastest growing Wisconsin cities is located just 20 minutes east of Minneapolis-St. Paul. Located high on a hill above the St. Croix River, the town first grew to importance in the lumber industry of the mid-1800s. The Octagon House, built in 1855, is maintained as a museum. Other attractions include the Phipps Center for the Arts and nearby Willow River State Park. In 2002, this city made the news when two funeral home workers were found murdered. A priest, who later committed suicide, is suspected of the crimes.

1	2	3	4		5	6	7	8	9		10	11	12	13
14					15						16			
17					18						19			
20			21			22		23		24				
		25		26	27		28			29				
30	31	32				33		34						
35				36			37		38		39	40	41	
42			43		44			45		46				
47				48		49			50		51			
		52		53		54				55				
56	57	58			59			60						
61				62		63			64		65	66	67	
68			69		70		71	72		73				
74					75					76				
77					78					79				

Across

1 An equal share
5 Adjust slightly
10 Paddles
14 Aroma
15 ___ Culture National Historic Park in New Mexico
16 Scheme
17 Volcanic flow
18 Emission of microwave radiation (abbr.)
19 DVR rival
20 Fix
22 Family lineage chart
24 London's Big ___
25 Shout
28 [Base hide], Wisconsin
30 [Soup eerier],Wisconsin
34 Unopened
35 Hudson to Rhinelander direction
36 Shish ___
38 "___ says"
42 And others (abbr.)
44 Type of detector
46 Bog
47 Upright
49 Saw socially
51 Sheltered side
52 Head movement
54 [Sure would], Wisconsin

56 [Belt chum], Wisconsin
60 Fourth Great Lake
61 ___ mode (2 wds.)
62 Tidy
64 Patio brick
68 Domed dwelling
70 Tempts
73 Magnitude
74 Rim
75 1996 Madonna movie
76 To be (Fr.)
77 Woodwind need
78 Settle an IOU
79 Portion of bread

Down

1 Spanish hello
2 First man
3 Adore
4 South of Luxembourg
5 Old movies channel (abbr.)
6 ___-TV, Wisconsin Public Television
7 ___ of Eden
8 Bitter
9 Southeast Asian war
10 Choose
11 Excuse
12 Wandered
13 *The Family* ___
21 Dim

23 Peepers
26 Actor Neeson
27 Divided
29 Cut through the water
30 Appear
31 "Do ___ others..."
32 Fruit tree
33 Roll calls
37 Get clean
39 Venus de ___
40 Black and white cookie
41 Requirement
43 Delafield-based company
45 Ogle
48 Cut of meat
50 Leak
53 Sword fighter
55 Mislead
56 Aspirin brand name
57 Out maneuver
58 Grand
59 Reddish hue
63 Journey
65 The Godfather's first name
66 Poet Pound
67 The Great Barrier ___
69 Singer Nugent
71 Airport info
72 What did you ___?

Solution on page 137.

Sound out the words under the "phonetic" name heading until you hear the common name of a Wisconsin city. The number and spacing of the blanks provide you with additional clues.

"Phonetic" Name   Common Name

1 Luck Raws   __ __   __ __ __ __ __ __

2 Kohl Facts   __ __ __ __ __ __

3 Kneels Fill   __ __ __ __ __ __ __ __ __ __

4 Add Dumbs   __ __ __ __ __

5 Prints Done   __ __ __ __ __ __ __ __

6 Saw Kiss Itty   __ __ __ __   __ __ __ __

7 Eke Cull   __ __ __ __ __

8 Marry Yawn   __ __ __ __ __ __

9 Rye Slake   __ __ __ __   __ __ __ __

10 Oak Couch He   __ __ __ __ __ __ __ __

Solution on page 136.

Scrambled below are the names of cities that declare themselves as world capitals in different arenas. Can you unscramble each name and then find them in the grid? As an aid to unscrambling, the city names are in alphabetical order. The scrambled city's claim to fame is listed across from it.

LELELELBIV	UFO Capital of the World
MOLBROE	Jump Rope Capital of the World
DONBLUE	Spelling Capital of the World
COBBLESO	Turkey Capital of the World
DOUBLER COTINJUN	Musky Capital of the World
DRUMBELACN	Rutabaga Capital of the World
ALGEE VIRRE	Snowmobile Capital of the World
WHERSOLLT	Cheese Curd Capital of the World
TROFENM	White Bass Capital of the World
SANGOLE	Brook Trout Fishing Capital of the World
DINGLED	Black Bear Capital of the World
REEGN YAB	Toilet Paper Capital of the World
CREEMR	Loon Capital of the World
NOORME	Swiss Cheese Capital of the World
NUTMO BROHE	Troll Capital of the World
WRAKONL	Black Squirrel Capital of the World
SLANAKOA	Sunfish Capital of the World
BOOX	Wood Tick Capital of the World
KARP SLALF	Ruffed Grouse Capital of the World
QUESPER SLEI	Walleye Capital of the World
CARNIE	Kringle Capital of the World
TRESSMOE	Inner Tubing Capital of the World
DAYTHAECHE	Sheepshead Fishing Capital of the World
ERAWSNR	Cranberry Capital of the World
USAUWA	Ginseng Capital of the World
MAUTAWO	Christmas Tree Capital of the World

Now take the cities you have unscrambled and find them in the grid below.

N	O	I	T	C	N	U	J	R	E	D	L	U	O	B
E	L	S	R	U	A	S	U	A	W	K	D	B	O	E
D	B	E	P	M	Q	R	N	O	I	L	U	S	E	L
D	D	Y	A	B	N	E	E	R	G	E	C	R	G	L
I	E	U	R	E	E	C	R	M	O	O	N	E	L	E
L	O	R	K	R	O	R	C	O	B	X	O	S	A	V
G	J	D	F	L	M	E	B	E	O	R	U	M	R	I
L	U	N	A	A	E	M	L	X	N	Q	O	R	E	L
E	C	E	L	N	T	W	U	O	D	T	S	R	W	L
A	I	T	L	D	S	A	M	W	U	M	O	E	N	E
S	O	N	S	S	R	R	Y	A	E	T	M	A	S	L
O	T	R	E	A	I	R	W	C	L	K	E	P	A	L
N	N	A	E	D	C	E	C	U	H	N	R	F	K	S
O	O	C	H	M	L	N	U	M	O	E	S	G	S	W
R	M	I	Y	A	O	S	A	Q	L	K	E	L	A	O
W	E	N	H	T	V	O	W	B	S	A	T	D	L	R
A	R	E	V	I	R	E	L	G	A	E	N	I	A	T
L	F	L	B	O	C	U	M	B	L	A	R	D	N	H
K	M	O	U	N	T	H	O	R	E	B	I	P	O	T

Wisconsin Lakes

Across

1 Kelly's co-host
6 Fat
10 Pool beginning
14 Archie's wife
15 Cookie for dunking
16 Nevada neighbor
17 Wood that floats
18 Wisconsin's largest inland lake
20 Dr.'s org.
21 Garlic mustard or purple loosestrife
23 Sign another lease
24 Katherine ___ (Henry VIII's last wife)
25 Slipped
27 One of the lakes creating Madison's isthmus
30 Poem with a hero
31 Hill inhabitant
34 San Antonio landmark
35 Dragon homes
36 Island neckwear
37 Speech impediment
38 Baseball's Yogi
39 Frat party wear
40 Actress Longoria
41 Mad
42 Forty-niner
43 Spice for French fries?
44 Morse code bit

45 Wisconsin lake once popular with Chicago elite
46 Promise
47 Actress Helen
48 Hide
51 ___ of milk and honey
52 Waking ___ Devine
55 Lake created by Prairie du Sac dam
58 Central Florida city
60 Locale
61 Pestered
62 Sum
63 Bull's opposite
64 Ride for kids
65 Torment

Down

1 Former CW TV show
2 Type of cheese
3 Monster starter
4 "___ all relative"
5 Northern Wisconsin lake popular with ice racers
6 Inferior
7 Like a desert
8 ___ and Stimpy
9 Put on
10 Cut in squares
11 And others
12 Wise man

13 Stroke in golf
19 Clapton and Carle
22 Time period
24 ___ and Circumstance
25 Church topper
26 Turkish money
27 Fathers, uncles, brothers
28 Italian cooking oil source
29 Midwestern accent quality
30 Between Mars and Venus
31 Solo
32 Desert in Israel
33 Crown
35 Dog walker's need
38 Staple on Wisconsin grills
39 Color hue
41 Nevada neighbor
42 One of the lakes creating Madison's isthmus
45 What Annie got
46 Writer Wilde
47 Good at fixing things
48 Cotton ___
49 Run out of gas
50 Sailing
51 Claim on a property
52 Intl. group created in 1949
53 Zeal
54 Golfer John
56 ___/Tuck
57 Hit movie sign (abbr.)
59 Sprocket

Solution on page 137.

Robin Level

1 Name the two Great Lakes that border Wisconsin.

2 What lake is the centerpiece for Wisconsin's most-visited state park?

3 Does Wisconsin have more than the 10,000 lakes that Minnesota boasts of?

Musky Level

4 Which is Wisconsin's deepest natural lake?

5 What is the meaning of Lake "Butte des Morts"?

6 What was the source of nearly all natural lakes in Wisconsin?

Badger Level

7 What is the most common name for a lake in Wisconsin?

8 Stone pyramids are believed to lie on the bottom of which Wisconsin lake?

9 Which Wisconsin county has the most lakes at 1,318?

Solution on page 136.

Wisconsin Lakes Revealed

The 10 lakes below are listed in alphabetical order. Read the descriptions that follow and try to match them to the Wisconsin lake they are describing.

Castle Rock Lake	**Lake Pepin**
Lake Chippewa Flowage	**Lake Winnebago**
Lake Geneva	**Lake Wisconsin**
Lake Koshkonong	**Lake Wissota**
Lake Mendota	**Turtle-Flambeau Flowage**

1 Located in Iron County, this lake is more than 13,000 acres and is a popular spot for fishing bluegill, bass, pike, and walleye. The minimum length on muskie here is 40 inches. Just southeast of Mercer, the lake was created by a 1926 dam to generate energy for a paper corporation. Technically there are nine lakes, three rivers, and a number of creeks incorporated here. Its nickname is the "Crown Jewel of Wisconsin."

2 At almost 14,000 acres, this lake is the fourth largest in Wisconsin. Located on the borders of Juneau and Adams Counties and a short drive north of Wisconsin Dells, it is fed by the Wisconsin River. Buckhorn State Park sits on a peninsula in the middle of the lake. A dam created the lake, just as a dam created Petenwell Lake, the state's second largest, directly north of it.

3 This lake is well-known for the resort communities that surround it. In the late 1800s, many wealthy Chicago families built grand mansions on its shores. The University of Chicago's Yerkes Observatory is perched high above the north shore. The area is now popular with pleasure boaters from the spas and golf resorts nearby.

4 This 6,000-plus acre lake lies close to Chippewa Falls and Eau Claire. A state park bearing its name is situated on its northeast shore. It was created by a man-made dam constructed by the Wisconsin-Minnesota Light and Power Company in 1917. The character Jack from the film *Titanic* mentions fishing on the lake as a boy, however, the *Titanic* sank in 1912, before the construction of the dam had even begun.

5 Although it is the largest lake (137,708 acres) in Wisconsin, its average depth is only 15 feet. It is a natural lake created by a glacier but supplemented by the construction of two dams in 1850. High Cliff State Park is the only state park that it touches. A county is named after this lake, but it borders three counties in total. The lake is known for its huge "ice shoves", when frozen lake ice pushes onto shore and bulldozes anything in its path.

6 At 25,000 acres, this lake is the widest natural section of the Mississippi River. In 1922, Ralph Samuelson invented water skiing on the lake. A fur trading post was built on its Minnesota shore in 1727. Ice roads over the lake connect the two states in winter. A city and county share its name. Laura Ingalls Wilder was born just a few miles from here.

7 As the biggest lake in Dane County at almost 10,000 acres, it borders one side of the isthmus on which our State Capitol is built. The University of Wisconsin-Madison lies along its south shore. The lake was the site of a prank in February 1979 when students constructed the top half of the Statue of Liberty on the ice, with its eyes, hand, and torch peeking above the surface of the lake. The long history of data taken on the lake's freeze and thaw dates has aided scientists studying global warming.

8 This spot claims to be Wisconsin's largest wilderness lake. The lake is technically made up of many smaller lakes and bays. The lake sits between the Lac Court Oreilles Indian Reservation and a portion of the Chequamegon-Nicolet National Forest in Sawyer County. The world-record 69-pound 11-ounce muskellunge was caught here, just a few miles from the famous Hayward Freshwater Fishing Hall of Fame, which is shaped like a giant muskie. Moose can often be seen near this lake.

9 This lake was created after completion of the Prairie du Sac Dam in 1924. The river side of the dam is a popular nesting ground for bald eagles in winter. Located in Columbia and Sauk Counties, the lake is popular with locals and tourists alike. A golf course of the same name lies to its south with its popular "island tee" sitting in the lake within view of the dam. Wisconsin's only free ferry operates farther northeast on the lake. The Merrimac Ferry has been taking passengers across these waters since 1844.

10 This Jefferson County lake was formed during the retreat of the glaciers at the end of the last ice age. Native Americans of the Woodland Period (1000 BC – 1300 AD) created hundreds of effigy mounds around the lake. A dam was built downstream of the lake in the mid 1800s, making this lake the second largest lake in the state at that time. Newer dams have dropped it down in the rankings. Much wildlife can be spotted here, including the occasional pelican.

Solution on page 136.

All the words below are names of lakes in Wisconsin. The words are encrypted in the same code. Can you break the code to read the names of all the lakes? As a solving aid, the words are listed in alphabetical order. For an extra hint, see the bottom of the page.

1 GKO GPII

2 GRYYLVWRY

3 JBLYLS

4 TLQYHW

5 TRYJB BHQQHE

6 LQSBPVY

7 BPQX CHHW

8 SLOHWIP

9 QKYYQL IY. OLVCPKW

10 CLYHWOP

11 CRISLQQRWOL

12 WHSHCKI

13 ZLEPRSLL

14 ZVLIDRL KIQL

15 ZRJSPEPF

16 IKWKIIKZZK

17 YHCPBPES

18 NLVCKQQKHW

19 EPRGLIP

20 EBKYL ZHYPYH

Hint: Number eleven is also the name of Wisconsin's state fish.

Solution on page 136.

Fill all empty squares so that the nine letters appear once in each row, column, and 3x3 box. The answer, reading across the middle row, will reveal a popular fishing lake in Oneida County.

				A			M	H
A		N	W				S	I
	M			S	H			
K		S	O		N		H	A
N	A		H		S	K		O
			K	H			O	
H	S				I	N		W
I	K			N				

Solution on page 138.

SPORTS & RECREATION

The old saying that "for everything there is a season" is quite true when it comes to sports in Wisconsin. In spring we hear the crack of the bat at Miller Park; with summer comes the smell of fresh cut grass on the golf course; fall colors in Wisconsin always include the Green and Gold; and winter brings the freezing temperatures necessary for snow skiers and ice fishermen.

For those who like to cheer for the home team, major league sports fans have the Packers, Brewers, and Bucks, while college fans have an array of teams, including the Big Ten's Badgers. For those who prefer to get out of the bleachers and participate themselves, Wisconsin has community leagues for team sports such as softball, volleyball, and bowling. For participants in solo sports, there are numerous venues for snowshoeing, kayaking, bicycling, and the like.

Many notable sports figures have called Wisconsin home, including Vince Lombardi, Barry Alvarez, Eric Heiden, and Alan Kulwicki. Community support for high school sports leaves no doubt that future legends are in the making in Wisconsin.

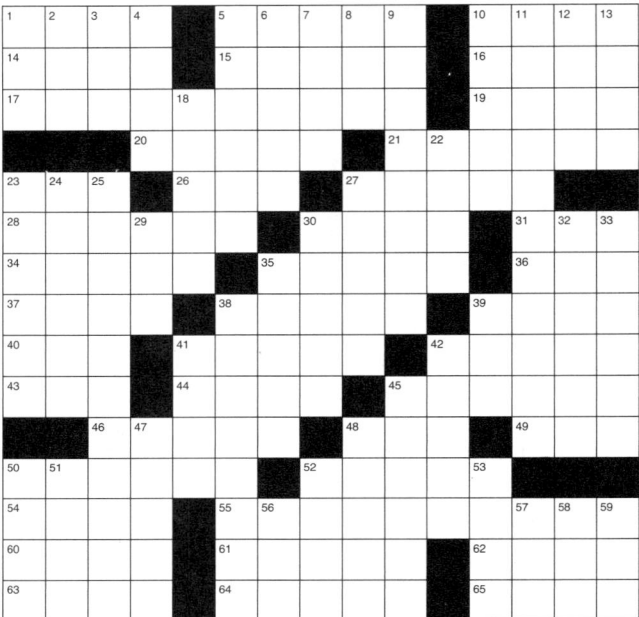

Across

1 Beach resident
5 Wedding site
10 Pre-wedding party
14 Boxer Oscar de la ___
15 Greek earth goddess
16 Volume
17 Wisconsin winter sport
19 Aid
20 German philosopher who inspired Karl Marx
21 Labor groups
23 Foot
26 Publicize
27 Informal language
28 Warm ocean current (2 wds.)
30 School bigwig
31 Satellite navigation network (abbr.)
34 Love
35 Designer Oscar de la ___
36 Southern constellation
37 Chops down
38 Birchbark vessel
39 Capture
40 Dangerous curve
41 Like a heron
42 Type of shot
43 To the ___ degree
44 United ___ Emirates
45 Immediately (2 wds.)

46 Playful swimmer
48 A vaccination (abbr.)
49 High school degree equivalent (abbr.)
50 Warns
52 Baseball coach ___ "Rod" Dedeaux
54 *Star Wars* Princess
55 Wisconsin winter sport (2 wds.)
60 Actor Sean
61 Singer John
62 Sticky substance
63 Groups (abbr.)
64 Clever
65 Singing voice

Down

1 22nd Greek letter
2 Mythical bird
3 Sailor's yes
4 Party
5 Slow, in music
6 Liquid amount
7 Labor
8 Columnist Landers
9 Govern
10 Mark
11 Wisconsin winter sport
12 Prayer closer

13 Receives
18 Family Circus creator Bill ___
22 Papa's mate
23 Female peacock
24 Most mature
25 Wisconsin winter sport
27 Address in Mexico
29 Auditing group (abbr.)
30 Brightest star in Cygnus
32 Sashay
33 Hung limply
35 Flying under the ___
38 Hugs
39 ___-mo instant replay
41 Lightbulb word
42 Thumb a guitar
45 Total
47 Type of fat
48 Important
50 Dog food brand name
51 Ogle
52 Ms. Moreno
53 Women's sporting organization (abbr.)
56 HIJ follower
57 Unwell
58 Madman
59 Earth (prefix)

Solution on page 137.

Robin Level

1 Wisconsinite Orson Welles directed and starred in the legendary film *Citizen Kane*. The mysterious "Rosebud" of the film turns out to be what winter sports equipment?

2 Which Wisconsinite won a long-awaited gold medal in speed skating at the 1994 Winter Olympics in Lillehammer in his last Olympic race?

3 Devil's Lake State Park's Ice Age Trail and Kettle Moraine State Forest's John Muir Trail are top locations for what winter sport?

Musky Level

4 What is the name for the hand drill that an ice fisherman uses to cut a hole through the ice?

5 What wintertime machine was invented in 1923 by Carl Eliason in Sayner, Wisconsin?

6 Which Wisconsin ski area is home to the highest vertical drop in Wisconsin?

Badger Level

7 What is the device used by ice fisherman to hold an unoccupied fishing pole?

8 West Allis, Wisconsin, is home to what world-renowned Olympic training facility?

9 The United States Curling Association's National Office is located in which Wisconsin city?

Solution on page 137.

A crossword puzzle grid with numbered cells.

Across

1 Actor Sandler
5 ___ machine
9 Wisconsin retiree Bonnie who won a record five gold medals
14 Cafeteria
15 Primo (hyph.)
16 Utah/Wyoming mountains
17 Property document
18 Algonquian language
19 Pave the driveway again
20 Blunder
21 Madisonian Eric who won five gold medals at Lake Placid
23 ___-de-France
24 Photographed again
27 ___, white, and blue
29 Verona native Casey who won a gold medal in Salt Lake City
35 Noodles
38 Name badges (abbr.)
39 Story
40 Apply
41 Shore
43 Actress Peeples
44 Not one
46 Cereal ingredient
47 Excited for
49 Olympic sport in which all these gold medals were won
53 Ready, ___, go!

54 Support
58 ___ Kapital
61 West Allis native Dan who won a gold medal in Lillehammer
64 Days of ___ Lives
65 Who Will You ___ (2 wds.)
67 Actress Paquin
68 Represented by a lightbulb
69 Farewell in France
70 Etiquette's Emily
71 Covers
72 West Allis native Chris who won a gold medal in Salt Lake City
73 Eyelid irritation
74 Common injury site

Down

1 Viper
2 Last name in tractors
3 Vigilant
4 Center
5 Perfumed bag
6 Nobel prize winner in medicine, 1973
7 The ___ Love, REM (2 wds.)
8 Propped up the ball
9 Scorched
10 Prevaricate
11 Con
12 Like this (abbr.)
13 Unusual

22 ___ & Young
25 Toward the stern
26 Sorento maker
28 ___-com business
30 Lariat
31 Commercials (abbr.)
32 Auld ___ syne
33 Bend in ballet
34 "Can you ___ me now?"
35 Witticisms
36 Now! (abbr.)
37 Withered
41 ___ Rica
42 Acorn's aspiration
45 Word of agreement
47 Conclusion
48 Past
50 Toile ___ fabric (2 wds.)
51 Very small
52 Nature, not nurture
55 French sculptor
56 Expensive skirt fabric
57 Rub out
58 Tie
59 Quattro maker
60 Tizzy
62 Afternoon rests
63 Prig
66 Vietnamese New Year
68 Sort

Solution on page 137.

Fill all empty squares so that the nine letters appear once in each row, column, and 3x3 box. The answer, reading across the middle row, will reveal the name for competitive curling matches.

Y			L					
		N			Y	P		O
	A			O			L	
D		S		N		O		Y
N		O		P		L		D
	P			W			Y	
W		L	O			S		
					P			W

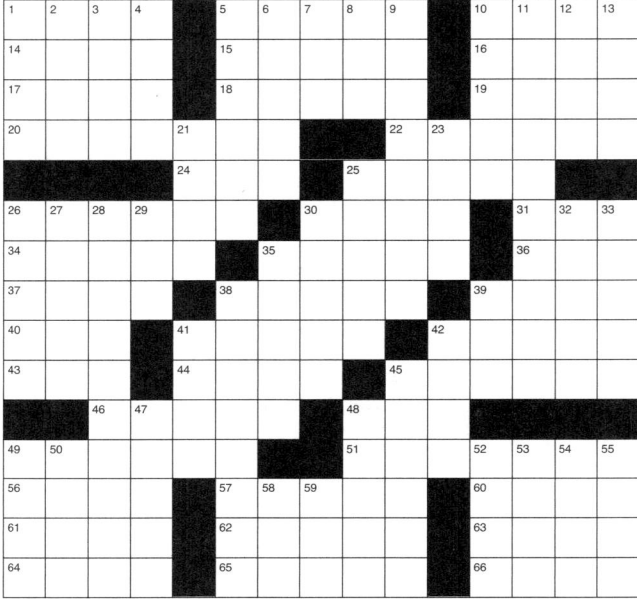

Across

1 Ladies
5 Work up a ___
10 Declare
14 Seed covering
15 Rhythm
16 Relocate
17 Farm's storehouse
18 Musician John
19 ___ du Salut (Safety Islands)
20 Location of the ski race known as the American Birkebeiner
22 Dairy offering
24 ___ Miserables
25 Faint
26 Another name for Inuit
30 Genius
31 Gentle knock
34 Uprisings
35 Rent
36 Huygens creator (abbr.)
37 Hamlet outside of Oshkosh
38 Its state animal is the moose
39 Not more
40 Period
41 Behind the times
42 French hat
43 Compass reading
44 Greek god of war
45 Nap
46 Relating to the moon

48 Opal is its birthstone (abbr.)
49 Where a skeleton might be kept
51 ___ 10K Family Fun Ski event
56 Between faith and charity
57 Therefore
60 ___ Major (The Great Bear)
61 Finished
62 Revulsion
63 Metrical unit for a poet
64 Dampens
65 ___ Dame
66 Colors

Down

1 Cut
2 Solo
3 Spring flower
4 Like a snail
5 Hi-fi
6 Joins by heat
7 Ambulance personnel (abbr.)
8 Address for armed forces (abbr.)
9 Founder of the American Birkebeiner (2 wds.)
10 Friend in Cancun
11 The American Birkebeiner couldn't be run without them
12 Happily ___ after
13 Pause
21 Donations

23 Leach
25 Classic book by Jack Schaefer
26 Wear away
27 American Idol judge Cowell
28 Name of the 23K ski event
29 Famous judge in the 90s
30 ___ beer (light-colored ale)
32 Attribute
33 Italian staple
35 Intense beam of light
38 The American Birkebeiner is North America's largest cross country ski ___
39 Robert E. ___
41 Window part
42 Chomp
45 Plan
47 Consumers
48 Happen
49 Fodder
50 Adore
52 ___ pro quo
53 Platter
54 Character from JD Salinger's Nine Stories
55 Research areas
58 Ancient name for Tokyo
59 Parasitic egg

Solution on page 139.

Across

1 Small tuft
5 Native Wisconsin shrub that can be poisonous
10 City in Italia
14 Fever from malaria
15 Domain
16 Actor Sitka, "The Fourth Stooge"
17 Balcony section
18 63-mile trail from Rice Lake to Superior (2 wds.)
20 Fishnet dragged through water
22 Beloved
23 Keanu's character in *The Matrix*
24 Actor-turned-activist Christopher
27 Halt
29 Concordant
32 2002 scare in Mid-Atlantic states
36 Three prefix
37 Side dish brand name
39 Ancient stone slab
40 Puppy ___
42 Oily type of acid
44 Picket-line crosser
45 Declares
47 Fable teller
49 ___ glance (2 wds.)
50 Angel of the first order

52 Carafe
54 1970s Billy Crystal TV show
56 Cowboy exhibition
57 "___-dah!" (Norwegian expression)
60 Vex
62 December 24th worker
65 24-mile state trail from Onalaska through Trempealeau (2 wds.)
69 Layer
70 Ogle
71 What a pilot may have to do in winter
72 Tan
73 Bark
74 Fourth deck
75 Pealed

Down

1 Disney or Whitman
2 Dr. Frankenstein's sidekick
3 23-mile state trail from New Glarus to Brodhead (2 wds.)
4 Half-pint
5 Buzz or chain follower
6 Psychic Geller
7 Blend
8 Where *Alive* took place
9 Jewel weights
10 Gun the engine
11 Harbinger

12 Wetland
13 Too
19 Does a dry cleaner's job
21 Scallion
25 Drink in 10 Across
26 1945's ___ Gay
28 Trenches
29 Rand McNally offering
30 Cottage ___ or Elm ___, WI
31 Avarice
33 10-mile state trail in Green County
34 Uplift
35 Steel used to reinforce concrete
38 Tread counterpart
41 Times
43 Ms. Chanel
46 "Be a good ___"
48 Cushions
51 Salon specialty
53 More cleanly
55 One who works at a trade
57 The ___ Duckling
58 ___ Willy
59 Sense
61 Word before eye or empire
63 Sea bird
64 Cut ___ (2 wds.)
66 A founder of Dada
67 Environment prefix
68 Agent (abbr.)

Solution on page 139.

37

Robin Level

1 What PGA player got his first career hole-in-one in his first PGA tournament at the Greater Milwaukee Open?

2 What world championship derby is held in Eagle River every year?

3 Name four of the five sausages in the Miller Park sausage races.

Musky Level

4 What gold-medal speed skater has a sister named Beth who won the 1980 world championship in Cycling-Road Race?

5 Wisconsinite Ed "Strangler" Lewis was the world champion in the 1920s and 30s for what sport?

6 In 1928, Harry Miller of Menomonie built what car part for nine of the top ten finishers in the Indy 500?

Badger Level

7 Black Creek, Wisconsin, claims to be the birthplace of the first organized national team for this sport.

8 The nation's two oldest sports facilities of this type are found at Holler House in Milwaukee.

9 Baseball in Lake Tomahawk becomes a unique challenge in the summer because the players wear these.

Solution on page 136.

Across

1 Open
5 Tic
10 Chore
14 Quarry
15 Sample
16 Actress Thompson
17 Ye ___ Shoppe
18 LPGA tour player Sherri from Madison, Wisconsin
20 Manner
22 Female singing voice
23 America's Uncle
24 *Tomorrow ___ Dies*
27 Parcel
28 Epoch
29 Former name of Zimbabwe
32 Johnny ___ (gray coat)
34 "___ the ramparts…"
35 Ashley and Wynonna's mother
37 Humble
41 Trail
43 Central New York city
45 Impulse
46 Quintessence
48 Cuts
50 *Monsters, ___.*
51 Agent (abbr.)
53 City just north of La Crosse
55 Clean the floor
58 ___ Cruces, NM
60 Ulysses S. ___

61 Mother of the ancient Irish gods
62 Throb
64 Hurly burly
67 PGA tour player from Madison (2 wds.)
71 Actress Sorvino
72 Holy Roman Emperor
73 Alleviated
74 "He's ___ up to his eyeballs" (2 wds.)
75 Dusty pink color
76 Backs into a corner
77 Eons

Down

1 Old Testament book
2 Cast aside
3 Two-time US Open Championship winner from Madison (2 wds.)
4 Staggered
5 Aves.
6 Touch playfully
7 On the water
8 Unmoving
9 Counselor
10 Drink of herbs or leaves
11 Entertain
12 Blotch
13 Belief of "getting what you deserve"

19 Inn
21 Fair
25 Jacob's twin
26 Calamities
29 Twine
30 Warmth
31 Type of acid
33 Curtsy
36 Frosting
38 ___ Straits, site of the 2004 PGA Championship near Kohler, Wisconsin
39 Connection
40 Activity club (abbr.)
42 Not his
44 On ___ (even) (2 wds.)
47 Type of race
49 Grand ___, winning the four biggest tournaments in golf
52 Bundle
54 Blood deficiency
55 Nickname for one of the four big golf tournaments
56 "…and ___ grow on" (2 wd.)
57 Sections
59 Cut the wool from a sheep
63 Additional
65 One of the Great Lakes
66 Consumes
68 Fish eggs
69 Robert E. ___
70 3-foot increments (abbr.)

Solution on page 139.

The grid (numbered cells):

```
 1  2  3  4  .  5  6  7  8  .  9 10 11 12 13
14  .  .  .  . 15  .  .  .  . 16  .  .  .  .
17  .  .  .  . 18  .  .  .  . 19  .  .  .  .
20  .  .  .  . 21  .  .  . 22  . 23  .  .  .
24  .  . 25 26  .  .  .  .  . 27  . 28  .  .
 .  .  . 29  .  .  .  . 30 31  .  .  . 32 33 34
35 36 37  .  .  . 38  .  .  . 39  .  .  .
40  .  .  . 41 42  .  .  .  . 43  .  .  .
44  .  .  . 45  . 46  .  .  . 47 48  .  .
49  .  .  . 50  .  .  . 51 52  .  .  .  .
 .  .  . 53  .  .  . 54  .  .  . 55 56 57
58 59 60  . 61  . 62 63  .  .  . 64  .  .
65  .  . 66  .  . 67  .  .  . 68  .  .  .
69  .  .  .  . 70  .  .  . 71  .  .  .  .
72  .  .  .  . 73  .  .  . 74  .  .  .  .
```

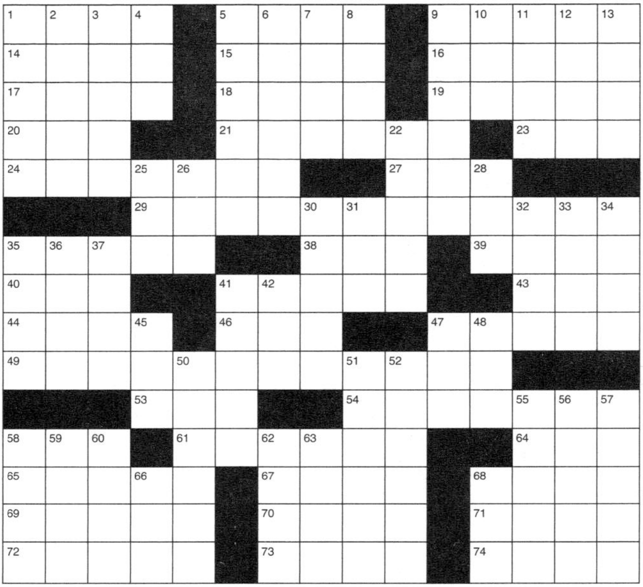

Across

1 Big ___ Golf Course, Hayward, designed by Pete Dye
5 Smolder
9 Educate
14 A single instance
15 Hot Apple product
16 Not on shore (2 wds.)
17 Steak order
18 Stretched
19 ___ Your Wagon
20 Card game
21 Governing body
23 Gobbled
24 Act as a go-between
27 Mr. Onassis
29 ___ Golf Club, Wisconsin Dells, designed by Andy North and Roger Packard (2 wds.)
35 Hearing or taste, for example
38 Common conjunction
39 Unwise twin
40 Actress Longoria
41 Like a beach
43 Military rank (abbr.)
44 City NNE of Lake Tahoe
46 Poetic tribute
47 "___ are red..."
49 ___ Golf Course, Kohler, designed by Pete Dye (2 wds.)
53 Sandal peeper
54 Type of novel

58 Psychic's claim (abbr.)
61 Like some lumber
64 Flub
65 Like some dates
67 Fast food order (2 wds.)
68 Moonstruck star
69 Church income source
70 Sound of the sea
71 Cookie for dipping in milk
72 Shaquille ___
73 Building additions
74 The ___ at Pinehurst Farms, Sheboygan Falls, designed by Jack Nicklaus

Down

1 Greek meeting place
2 Ridiculous
3 Young Atlantic cod
4 ___ Haw
5 Party in Madrid
6 Maintenance
7 Kohler rival
8 Old Icelandic work of myth
9 Slender candles
10 Mitchell Field stat
11 Home to Mt. Everest
12 Penny
13 10 Things I ___ about You
22 Late
25 ___ a Wonderful Life
26 "Violets ___ blue..."

28 Wisconsin ending
30 Jury
31 Finish
32 Federal agency (abbr.)
33 Dance party
34 Crazy
35 Certain Slavic person (abbr.)
36 Daredevil Knievel
37 Grandma
41 Planter
42 Bustle
45 Canadian Thanksgiving month (abbr.)
47 Liquor made from molasses
48 "___ lighter note..." (2 wds.)
50 Newsman Ted
51 Tight-fisted
52 Helicopter blades
55 First Prime Minister of India
56 Wicker fishing basket
57 Actor Flynn
58 Outer (prefix)
59 Lower leg portion
60 Seeger or Sampras
62 To be (Fr.)
63 Rad
66 Words of discovery
68 Corn on the ___

Solution on page 139.

Fill all empty squares so that the nine letters appear once in each row, column, and 3x3 box. The answer, reading across the middle row, will reveal the name of a golf course in Oregon, WI, designed by Andy North.

	N	E			G	B	R	
	B	O		N	E			G
	G	N		T		R	B	
	T	M		B		G	A	
G			R	O		A	E	
	R	A	T			N	M	

Robin Level

1 Name the former location for home Badger basketball games before the Kohl Center.

2 What is the name given to the UW Marching Band's performance after football games?

3 Name one of the two Badger football players who went on to win the Heisman.

Musky Level

4 Name two of the three years the Badgers have won the Rose Bowl.

5 Name eight of the thirteen sports in the Badger's athletic program.

6 What did the Badger Women's Hockey Team accomplish in 2006 and 2007?

Badger Level

7 What is the full name of UW Madison's mascot?

8 How many times has the Badger Men's Hockey Team won the NCAA Hockey Championship?

9 What is the only year in which the Badger Men's Basketball Team won the NCAA Championship?

Solution on page 137.

Badgers in the Wisconsin Athletic Hall of Fame

All the words below are names of Badgers who are in the Wisconsin Athletic Hall of Fame. The names are encrypted in the same code. Can you break the code to read the names of all the Badgers? As a solving aid, the words are listed in alphabetical order. For an extra hint, see the bottom of the page.

1 QXQ AXLGCXG

2 ELIVC CZYVGRYZF

3 ELMEN BYGCNY

4 HKPVH CELIYVGYI

5 HXG TYLIRKGG

6 HXG NVGHZ

7 YWIXO LVICEL

8 TYXITY SXKTY

9 TMO CMGHZ

10 LKIWKG IXTYIC

11 LKIXWH "QMH" BXCZYI

12 LXDKIH QMEN

13 VPKG DVWWVKRCXG

14 AXLG RYCCRYI

15 RKIWVG "SKZ" LKIHYI

16 SKZ IVELZYI

17 SKZIVEN X'HYK

18 IXWWVY DVWWVKRC

19 ZLXRKC AXGYC

20 DKWZYI RYKGDYWW

Hint: Number seven's nickname was Crazy Legs.

Solution on page 137.

The Green Bay Packers

Across
1 Play a horn
5 Evergreen tree
10 ___ ghanoush
14 Maker of the Cabriolet
15 Bring together
16 Having wings
17 Young chaps
18 ___ Valley National Park
19 The good old ___
20 Pondered
22 *What ___ Beneath*
24 Pasture sound
25 Scallion
28 Packers' co-founders Curly Lambeau and George ___
30 Kid-supplied modes of transportation for Packer players to the practice field
34 Two o'clock beverage
35 Tropical blackbird
36 Indian maids
38 Anger
42 Look over
44 Ancient stone slab with markings
46 ___ mater
47 Holler
49 Look after (2 wds.)
51 Scab
52 ___ *Doubtfire*
54 "Green Bay Packers" is the longest standing ___ in NFL history (2 wds.)

56 Nickname of the famous 1967 Packers' game (2 wds.)
60 Ballet bend
61 Resurfacing material
62 Shipbuilding wood
64 Lock of hair
68 ___ go bragh
70 All of the ___
73 Egotistical
74 Sceptre
75 Creed
76 Writer Bombeck
77 Data on an athlete
78 Chalkboard material
79 Undergarment

Down
1 Soothing substance
2 Hawaiian feast
3 Wagering info
4 With sound judgment
5 What a cow chews
6 Janesville to Milwaukee direction
7 Feature of a rotary phone
8 Storage space
9 Use a microwave
10 Leroy Brown quality
11 San Antonio attraction
12 Water feature in the Deep South
13 Fireman's bane

21 Ten (prefix)
23 Heap
26 *Desire Under the ___*
27 *Ode to a Nightingale* author
29 Arduous
30 Largemouth fish
31 "A pinch to grow an ___"
32 Italian greeting
33 Linen closet item
37 8-hour activity
39 Halo
40 Miner transportation
41 Type of speech
43 Stunned
45 And others (abbr.)
48 Move like a horse
50 Leave out
53 Comfy clothes
55 Get on someone's ___
56 List members
57 Unit of weight
58 *All My Children's* Kane
59 Classify
63 Hawaiian winter wind
65 Ranking above a Viscount
66 California valley
67 Sound made with fingers and thumb
69 Profit
71 Animal doc
72 Riviera summer

Solution on page 140.

Robin Level

1 What is the name given to the celebration players make when they join fans in the stands of Lambeau Field after a touchdown?

2 Who did the Packers beat in Superbowl XXXI?

3 Who owns the Packers?

Musky Level

4 Who was the Packers' Vice President and General Manager from 1991-2001?

5 Name three of the five Packer players whose jerseys have been retired.

6 Brett Favre completed his first career pass to which player?

Badger Level

7 What road connects Brett Favre Pass to Lombardi Avenue?

8 Who is the only player to ever have worn jersey #1 for the Packers?

9 Who did the Packers beat in Superbowl I?

Solution on page 137.

The Green Bay Packers Quiz

How much do you really know about the Green and Gold? Can you tell which of the following 20 items are fact or fiction? Mark a T for true and an F for false.

1 The original members of the Green Bay Packers were from a meat packing company named Indian Packing, later to be named Acme Packing.

2 The Packers are the third oldest team in the NFL (formerly the American Professional Football Association).

3 The Packers hold a record 12 championship titles.

4 Salaries for the 1919 Packer players were paid for through money collected in a hat that was passed among fans during halftime.

5 A financial blow involving a lawsuit stemming from a bleacher accident and an injured spectator almost brought an end to the Packers during the Depression.

6 Vice President Richard Nixon attended the dedication of the new City Stadium in September 1957.

7 Future serial killer Randall Woodfield was drafted by the Green Bay Packers in 1973. However, he was let go in 1974 after a string of arrests for indecent exposure.

8 The first Packers game to be broadcast on television was in 1953.

9 The team's unofficial nicknames have included: Indians, Acme Packers, Blues, and Bays.

10 The original football field that the Packers played on was named Hagemeister Park.

11 Every Packers home game has been sold out since 1960.

12 The Green Bay Packers' fight song is *Go! You Packers! Go!*

13 There are about 71,500 people on the waiting list for season tickets for the Packers, which equals about a 35-year wait.

14 Green Bay Coach Vince Lombardi was on the cover of *Time* magazine in December 1962.

15 The Green Bay Packers and the Chicago Bears have played each other more times than any other two teams in NFL history.

16 The Packers' public Hall of Fame was the first of its kind in the NFL.

17 In the Commander Keen video game series, the main character, Billy Blaze (a.k.a. Commander Keen), wears a Green Bay Packers football helmet.

18 Former Packer backup quarterback Matt Hasselbeck has been struck by lightning twice.

19 Starting with the Green Bay Packers in Super Bowl XXXII in 1998, the NFC team has won the coin toss at the Super Bowl for ten straight years in a row.

20 No individual is allowed to hold more than 200,000 shares in the Green Bay Packers.

Solution on page 137.

Vince Lombardi Quotes

Vince Lombardi is arguably one of the best-known figures in NFL history, let alone a Green Bay Packer legend. In his nine years as the head coach of the Packers, he led the team to five NFL championship wins. His national fame led Richard Nixon to consider Lombardi as a running mate for his 1968 bid for the presidency; however, Lombardi was a Democrat. Lombardi died of cancer in 1970. A week after his death, the NFL's Super Bowl trophy was named the Vince Lombardi Trophy in his honor and is still called that today.

Lombardi was known for his utter dedication, vigorous motivational skills, and philosophic look at the game of football. The quote for which he is the most famous is "Winning isn't everything, it's the only thing." The authenticity of the exact words is somewhat in dispute, and he regretted that the sentiment was attributed to him, saying, "I wish to hell I'd never said the damned thing. I meant having a goal.... I sure as hell didn't mean for people to crush human values and morality."

To learn some of his authentic quotes about football, which he called "a game that requires the constant conjuring of animosity," and about life, read the instructions for the different types of puzzles to solve.

Scrambled Words: In the puzzles below, the words are in the right order but the letters in each word are all mixed up. Unscramble the letters in each word to reveal the quote.

1 HET CRIPE FO CESCUSS SI RADH KORW, HTE RETENTADIMNIO HATT HEWRETH EW NWI RO SOLE, EW VAHE DEPLIPA EHT STEB FO SOURVELES OT HTE SAKT TA NAHD.

2 EW NTIDD SELO HET MEAG; EW STUJ NAR UTO F O MITE.

3 STI TON HERTHEW UOY ETG DOKKENC WNOD, TIS TREWHEH OYU GTE PU.

4 EW DOLUW CASHLIMPCO NYAM ROME GISHTN FI EW IDD TNO KIHNT FO MEHT SA POBISLIMSE.

Solution on page 139.

5 KOTRAMEW SI ATHW EHT ENEGR YAB RACEKSP
REEW LAL TAUBO. EHYT NTIDD OD TI RFO
UNVIADIDLI RYGOL, YHET IDD TI SCEABUE HYTE
DELOV NEO TREANOH.

Cryptoquote: Find the letter substitution code to read the quote.
For example, if POGNP stood for TRUST, all the other Ps in the puzzle
stand for Ts, and so forth. The code is different for all five puzzles.

1 KROOROM RF OBQ L FBPJQRPJ QAROM; RQ'F LO
LEE QRPJ QAROM. DBZ SBO'Q KRO BOYJ RO L K
AREJ, DBZ SBO'Q SB QAROMF WRMAQ BOYJ RO
L KAREJ, DBZ SB QAJP WRMAQ LEE QAJ QRPJ.
KROOROM RF ALVRQ. ZOCBWQZOLQJED FB
RF EBFROM.

2 WJ HYM QTSK'Z JWTSB UWZP SKZPMFWQFD, HYM
UWRR IS JWTSB UWZP SKZPMFWQFD.

3 R CNKFFA HVGKFPG UFFGORAA VC VW
ERWSJM FU EJGJMVFMRGVWS VWGF R
QJEVJZRA CGPEL KRAA.

4 ECL GNRRLILHOL JLEPLLH S XMOOLXXRMW VLIX
TH SHG TECLIX NX HTE S WSOA TR
XEILHYEC HTE S WSOA TR AHTPWLGYL
JME ISECLI S WSOA TR PNWW.

5 WTRWFT BSR BRON CRHTCSTO BMFF BME BSTC
STO MC UT JHJMEVC KRXWFTQ
LRRCUJFF ITLTEVTV RO CST WORUFTXV
RL XRITOE VRKMTCZ.

Green Bay Packers Coaches

Across

1 ___ League, est. 1946
5 Aroma
9 Playwright Henrik
14 Pop
15 Hoarfrost
16 Small town in IA, UT, or WV
17 English prep school
18 Saga
19 ND city and name of a dark comedy film
20 Take care of (2 wds.)
22 Brass wind instrument
24 Funnyman Conway
25 Beers
28 Packers coach Gene from 1950-1953
30 Packers coach Mike from 1992-1998
34 Dined
35 Whichever
36 ___ on the wrist (2 wds.)
38 What Krakatoa can do
42 Cools
44 ___ the Cow
46 Scandinavian capital
47 Pauses
49 Chips sidekick
51 Very long time
52 I see!
54 Packers coach Vince from 1959-1967
56 Packers coach Earl from 1921-1949

60 Pre adult
61 Uganda dictator Amin
62 Level
64 Name
68 Poison
70 Not ___ many words (2 wds.)
73 Temper
74 Santa ___ Canyon, Big Bend National Park
75 Popular wood for patio furniture
76 "Look ___, I'm Sandra Dee" (2 wds.)
77 Auto
78 Morays
79 Tilt

Down

1 High cards
2 Memorization
3 ___ vera
4 Diminutive
5 Hematite, e.g.
6 Immerse
7 Leave out
8 Happen again
9 Packers coach Lindy from 1988-1991
10 Arthur from *Golden Girls*
11 Kinda
12 IL city on the Fox River
13 Ruth's mother-in-law
21 Gymnast Korbut

23 ___ constrictor
26 Celtic language
27 Vends
29 Nil
30 Tresses
31 A single time
32 Soap ingredients
33 Midwestern accent quality
37 Airplane VIP
39 Consumer
40 Trudge
41 Author Morrison
43 Attempt
45 Ms. Squalor of Lemony Snicket books
48 Packers coach Mike from 2000-2005
50 Assist
53 Travel group
55 Before instinct or magnetism
56 Exists
57 Fred Astaire's older sister
58 Excavated
59 Join
63 ___ jerk reaction
65 Carry
66 ___ Linda, CA
67 Paradise
69 ___ wing and a prayer (2 wds.)
71 Actor Mineo
72 Approves (abbr.)

Solution on page 140.

Wisconsin Stock-Car Racing Venues

Across

1 Glide
6 Pinkish color
11 Russian space station
14 Door fastener
15 Mimicry
16 *Men ___ from Mars...*
17 Au revoir
18 ___ Speedway, Cambridge
20 Director Craven
21 Persons, places, and things
23 ___ *It Romantic*
24 Adam's home
25 Electric guitarist's need
27 ___ Bay, Door County
30 *Beetle Bailey* dog
32 Walkie talkies
35 Grouch of reknown
36 David Cobb's party
37 Supermodel Carol
38 A man of the ___
39 Tattle
40 Type of rocky slope
42 Baseballer Griffey Jr.
43 Furious
45 Sum
46 Sault ___ Marie
47 Ear part
48 Rebuke
49 Tissue layer
50 Veer

51 Word before Bell or John's
54 Hide
56 Fuel
59 ___ Speedway, Wausau (2 wds.)
62 Love
64 Steve Case was its CEO
65 One over par
66 Word from a song
67 Motor speed (abbr.)
68 Buffalo kin
69 City on the River Aire in England

Down

1 Imperfection
2 Place a burden on
3 Name seen in elevators
4 Top gun
5 ___ Raceway, Sturgeon Bay
6 New Orleans specialty
7 Ajar
8 Game VIPs
9 Dog bark
10 Potassium hydroxide solution
11 Density times volume
12 It can be pumped
13 What an apartment dweller must do
19 Tombstone initials

22 *Star Spangled Banner* contraction
24 Les ___ Unis
25 "The dog ___ my homework"
26 ___ Raceway, Unity (2 wds.)
27 Punches
28 Small body of land
29 British pastry
30 Give a speech
31 Head (Fr.)
32 Magna ___
33 Sheep's cry
34 Ancient stone slab
36 Snag
41 Before pipe or cob
44 Actor Rogers
48 It could be city or school
49 "It all went to ___"
50 "This seat's ___"
51 Russian emperor
52 Over
53 Tranquil
54 Droops
55 Wise men, for example
56 Author of *Earth in the Balance*
57 Dry
58 60 make a min.
60 Recede
61 Hawaiian dish
63 Color

Solution on page 140.

Alan Kulwicki Quotes

Born in Greenfield, Wisconsin, Alan Kulwicki chased his dream of becoming a NASCAR driver. In 1986 he won the Winston Cup Rookie of the Year award. In 1992 he became the Winston Cup Champion. He was known for his "Polish Victory Lap" in which he would drive backward around the track. Tragically, Kulwicki died in April 1993 in a plane crash. In 2005, the movie *Dare to Dream* was made about his life.

Scrambled Words: In the puzzle below, the words are in the right order but the letters in each word are all mixed up. Unscramble the letters in each word to reveal the quote.

1 STRIF OYU NEARL OT VIDER STAF. XTEN, UOY RENAL OT RIVED SATF NI FRATFCI. HENT, YUO ARNEL WHO OT OD TI ROF VIFE DRUNHED SMILE.

2 FI OUY TOND VILEBEE YUO OTND GLOBEN.

Cryptoquote: Find the letter substitution code to read the quote. For example, if POGNP stood for TRUST, all the other Ps in the puzzle stand for Ts, and so forth. The code is the same for all three puzzles.

1 Z POBW O SLVVL: DLCI VL JWHLSW, RLV VL OHKMZCW.

2 Z YZYR'V DLCI VL DZR O SZAAZLR YLAAOCF, Z DL CIWY VL JWHLSW DZRFVLR HMU HPOSUZLR.

3 ZR WBWCX OFUWHV LE AZEW, POBW O NOSW UAOR, ORY VPWR YL XLMC JWFV VL OHPZWBW ZV.

Across

1 Word on a light bulb
5 Singer George
11 Droop
14 Most populous continent
15 Spins
16 Mutt
17 "America's Winningest Driver" from Wisconsin Rapids (2 wds.)
19 Uranium, for example
20 Poetry muse
21 Male deer
22 Newsman Donaldson
25 ___ and outs
26 Green flag signal
29 Knelt in a pew
31 Mole, for example
34 Doled out a PG or R
35 Short
36 Altar words
37 ___ and crafts
38 The best of the best
39 Austen novel
40 Asian ox
41 Smooths out
42 Office notes
43 Silver modifier
45 Gift
46 Unclothed
47 Plead
48 Streets (abbr.)
49 Have to

51 TV's Dr. Bob
53 Milwaukee to Detroit direction
54 NASCAR Craftsman Truck racer from Franklin (2 wds.)
60 Congeal
61 Type of newspaper column
62 Norse god
63 Pale hue
64 Showed agreement
65 Title

Down

1 Heap
2 *As Long ___ Live* (2 wds.)
3 Spasm
4 Accept
5 Wisp
6 Airheads
7 Puerto ___
8 Biblical craft
9 Sick
10 Mao ___ Tung
11 NASCAR Nextel Cup racer from Wausau (2 wds.)
12 Ambiance
13 Swimmer Louganis
18 ___ and true method
21 Theater sign (abbr.)
22 Paints, in a way
23 Biblical mount
24 Final Winston Cup winner from Cambridge (2 wds.)

26 It ___ him to a T
27 Conifer, for example
28 Bark
30 Affirmative
31 Carry
32 Astronomer Halley
33 Cooks a turkey
35 Marilyn Monroe quality
38 Buffalo's Lake
39 Snakey swimmer
41 Sort
42 The legend of Gog and ___
44 Squeal
45 Became taut
47 ___ *Almighty*
49 Western land formation
50 Employs
51 Between
52 Marched
54 Sun-kissed
55 AKA Tokyo
56 Movie rental format
57 Fruit juice drink
58 Compete
59 The ___

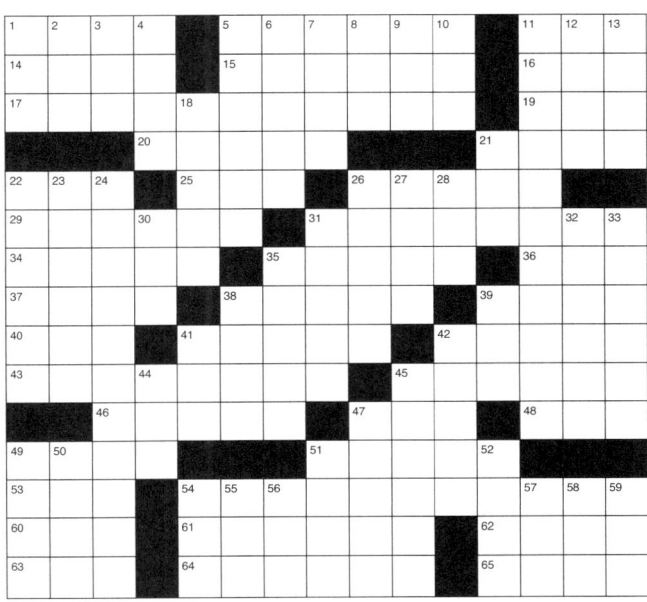

Solution on page 140.

THE GREAT OUTDOORS

Millions of people enjoy Wisconsin's state conservation and recreation lands each year. State parks, forests, trails, and wildlife areas allow residents and nonresidents alike to get back to nature. More than 15,000 lakes offer plenty of fishing, and six million acres of hunting land are available to bag that deer or turkey.

Wisconsin is bordered by two of the five Great Lakes, and centuries-old lighthouses dot the shore as a reminder of the state's seafaring past. In Lake Superior at Wisconsin's northernmost point lies the Apostle Islands National Lakeshore, one of the few lands in Wisconsin under the domain of the National Park Service.

The rich landscape, with its forests, valleys, lakes, and rolling hills, has been shaped by the extremes of weather that Mother Nature brings to our state. The flora and fauna have found harmony with Wisconsin's harsh winters, hot humid summers, and rainy seasons. Weather extremes, from blizzards to tornadoes, have tested the mettle of all Wisconsin's living creatures.

All the words below are names of state forests in Wisconsin. The answers are encrypted in the same code. Can you break the code to read the names of all the state forests? As a solving aid, the words are listed in alphabetical order. For an extra hint, see the bottom of the page.

1 UOQLT XRYWX

2 UXCOW XRYWX

3 LBCOWW WMSWXRGWVJQO

4 KOQGUWQC

5 PBYWXVBX TVBIOWH

6 AQYWVIBBFH

7 TWJJOW GBXQRVW

8 VBXJAWXV ARPAOQVF-QGWXRLQV OWPRBV

9 SWHAJRPB XRYWX

10 SBRVJ UWQLA

Hint: The word repeated three times in the puzzle is a body of water.

Solution on page 140.

Across

1 To impede
6 First five books of the Bible
11 Everything
14 Defendant's story
15 Often-fatal virus
16 Miss Piggy's pronoun
17 Cloak
18 Rib Mountain State Park was created from these two types of rock that are slower to erode than their surroundings (with 59 Across)
20 Go below the horizon
21 Records
23 Pennsylvania port city
24 Dusty pink
25 Choose
27 Backwater
30 Remove
32 Bush brother
35 Looking forward (to)
36 Found in a loo
37 One (Fr.)
38 Act of 1974 protecting retirement assets (abbr.)
39 Charged particle
40 Mrs. Gorbachev
42 Gun the engine
43 Elite shoe and handbag maker
45 Happen
46 Fond du Lac to Milwaukee direction (abbr.)
47 Watering device

48 Assented
49 Eau Claire to Stevens Point direction (abbr.)
50 Word after North or barber
51 Taj Mahal site
54 Peanut butter's partner
56 ___-Fi Channel
59 See 18 Across
62 Dress fold
64 Baseball ref
65 Grilling stick
66 Equine
67 Carl Sagan's subj. (abbr.)
68 Uncaps
69 Vapor

Down

1 Dines
2 Move sideways
3 Hue
4 Japanese sash
5 Roche-A-Cri State Park is one of the few places in the US where these carvings and paintings are seen side by side (with 26 Down)
6 Home to ASU
7 Contrabassoon
8 Director Howard and Baseball player Santo
9 Pie ___ mode (2 wds.)
10 It ___ to be You
11 Love in Spain
12 Sites

13 Enjoy
19 Butterfly catcher
22 Second most common urban tree in Wisconsin
24 Regrets
25 Grand ___ Opry
26 See 5 Down
27 Wise men
28 Household spirits in ancient Rome
29 Nose cone
30 Semiconductor
31 Wisconsinite author Ferber
32 Morning drink
33 Carry on
34 Facial hair
36 Prejudice
41 Plot of land
44 Caviar
48 Popular Internet group
49 Sense organ
50 Roman word for common people
51 Blue hue
52 Gingivitis locale
53 Engrossed
54 Aggressive remark
55 Prince William's alma mater
56 Without moisture
57 Home in Spain
58 Tidbit
60 Ring decision (abbr.)
61 Jolt
63 Home-building site

Solution on page 141.

Wisconsin State Parks

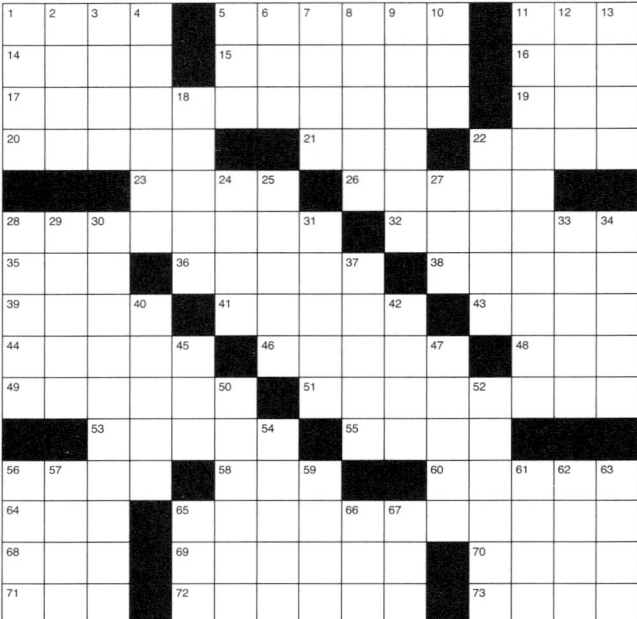

Across
1 Injury reminder
5 "I'm a little ___..."
11 Paid athlete
14 First Lady of Song's first name
15 Chocolate bar add-on
16 "___ the ramparts..."
17 State park near Mellen containing the Bad River (2 wds.)
19 Caffeinated beverage
20 Ruin
21 Atmosphere
22 Short antonym
23 Flair
26 Crooked
28 After George or before Ford
32 SE Mexico city and state
35 Gold in 32 across
36 Tennis player Monica
38 Before tot
39 Division
41 Courtyards
43 Cola
44 Not a giver
46 Odds' partner
48 Actress Ryan
49 Safe place
51 Latter part of the day (poetic)
53 Modify
55 Pitcher

56 Respiratory disease discovered in 2003
58 Inlet
60 Looking at
64 Sphere
65 State park near Hudson with a beach on Little Falls Lake
68 City in Brazil and Wisconsin
69 Indian Tribe of Wisconsin
70 Part of a church
71 What Van Gogh sliced off
72 Word before child
73 Chew

Down
1 Shorter than mins.
2 Horse hoof sound
3 Food for Fido
4 Sword
5 What you do before you feather?
6 North Pole inhabitant
7 Latin verb for love
8 Wisconsin state dance
9 Good looks can take you ___ far (2 wds.)
10 Badgers' scores (abbr.)
11 State park on the shore of Sturgeon Bay
12 Fisher's need

13 Spoken
18 Island in New York
22 Amarillo's state
24 Not ashore
25 Actor Nick
27 Kit ___
28 Shade-loving plant
29 Regions
30 State park near Wisconsin Dells with sandstone bluffs
31 Guts
33 Yielded
34 In ___ (irate, 2 wds.)
37 Strainer
40 Makes known
42 Once again
45 Slump
47 Villain's expression
50 Noted wool
52 Making an effort
54 Irritates
56 Tender
57 Solo
59 Landed
61 September 2004 hurricane
62 Russian river
63 Increased
65 Doo-___ (style of music)
66 Tribute poem
67 Conflict

Solution on page 141.

Robin Level

1 Mirror Lake State Park is the only state park in which you can rent a cottage designed by what famous Wisconsinite?

2 What is the largest and most popular state park in Wisconsin?

3 Blue Mound State Park is the only state park in Wisconsin with this type of aquatic recreational facility.

Musky Level

4 At Amnicon Falls State Park you can view the Douglas ___, where earthquakes rocked this land millions of years ago.

5 What type of overnight shelter is available to rent at Kohler-Andrae State Park?

6 The practice of cannibalism by ancient peoples has been suggested in artifacts found at this state park.

Badger Level

7 In which state park will you find the oldest cemetery in Wisconsin, with Indian burial grounds dating back 6,000 years?

8 This state park in southwestern Wisconsin has a name that comes from a Native American word meaning "home of the warriors."

9 Dedicated in 2005, this Polk County property is Wisconsin's newest state park.

Solution on page 140.

Wisconsin State Parks Revealed

The 10 state parks below are listed in alphabetical order. Read the descriptions that follow and try to match each to the Wisconsin state park it describes.

Blue Mound State Park   **Kohler-Andrae State Park**
Copper Falls State Park   **Peninsula State Park**
Devil's Lake State Park   **Rib Mountain State Park**
High Cliff State Park   **Rock Island State Park**
Interstate State Park   **Wyalusing State Park**

1 This state park lies at the northern tip of Door County. It is accessible by boat only. Neither cars nor bikes are allowed in the state park. The park is home to Wisconsin's first federal lighthouse, the Pottawatomie Lighthouse. Another structure, the Viking Boathouse, greets visitors with its impressive stone construction.

2 Established in 1900, this is Wisconsin's oldest state park. Its glacier-carved rock features are a highlight of the park, including the Dalles of the St. Croix. The western end of the Ice Age Trail lies inside this park. This state park, which Wisconsin shares with Minnesota, was the first in the United States to incorporate lands of two states.

3 Lying along the shore of Lake Michigan, this state park includes forested land, beaches, and sand dunes. Sometimes mass die-offs of white fish on the beach can drive visitors slightly inland, where long boardwalks meander among the dunes and grasses. Many shipwrecks occurred in this area in the 1800s. A portion of an 87-foot schooner named the *Challenge* washed ashore here and is now on display outside the Sanderling Nature Center.

4 The most popular state park in Wisconsin was created by great glaciers 13,000 years ago. Effigy mounds dating back a thousand years can be found inside the park. More recently, Ho-Chunk Indians used the area as a fishing village. Fancy resorts operated on the land in the late 1800s. Later uses included quarries, a golf course, and a toboggan slide. The site is now popular with swimmers, fishermen, campers, cross-country skiers, and rock scramblers.

5 This state park is found at the confluence of the Wisconsin and Mississippi rivers. Hiking up the bluffs leads to overlooks of the vast river delta lands below. Some of the other highlights include caves, an observatory, and effigy mounds. The park houses a monument whose plaque reads, "Dedicated to the last Wisconsin passenger pigeon shot at Babcock, Sept. 1899. This species became extinct through the avarice and thoughtlessness of man."

6 The North Country National Scenic Trail, which will eventually span from New York to North Dakota, runs through this state park. The Bad River tumbles northward over lava rock and into deep gorges carved by glaciers. The park is thick with wildlife: Deer, fishers, black bears, and red squirrels are often spotted here. Gray wolf sightings also occur. Recreation includes mountain bike trails and a 300-foot sand beach where swimmers can frolic in Loon Lake.

7 The highest hill in southern Wisconsin can be found within this state park. Observation towers flank either end of the picnic area and provide views all the way to the Baraboo bluffs. Niagara dolomite is the rocky earth underfoot here; its hardness has kept it from eroding down like the land surrounding it. The park is part of the Driftless Area, left untouched by the glaciers that ringed it.

8 This state park is probably best known for Granite Peak, a site for downhill skiing. The hilltop here is made of billion-year-old rock. A 60-foot tower crowns the top of one of the park's highest points. The park does not house the highest point in Wisconsin, but it does include the tallest hill, at 700 feet above the surrounding plain. In the summer, the free musical series, "Concerts in the Clouds," is staged in the park's amphitheater.

9 This state park lies on the Niagara Escarpment, a limestone cliff on the eastern side of Lake Winnebago. The ledge extends all the way to Niagara Falls, New York. Views of Wisconsin's largest lake and the Fox Valley area are enhanced by a 40-foot observation tower. The remnants of a limestone kiln can still be seen on the property today, a reminder of its past as a busy quarry.

10 From the shore of Green Bay to the rocky bluffs above, this park has numerous features in between. Take a tour of Eagle Bluff Lighthouse, play 18 holes of golf, kayak out to Horseshoe Island, or watch the professional thespians performing at American Folklore Theater. Wintertime means snowshoeing, cross-country skiing, ice fishing, snowmobiling, and sledding. Myriad tourist attractions exist nearby, including restaurants and antique shopping.

Solution on page 141.

State Wildlife Areas

Across

1 Official records
5 Ceremonial pole
10 What a waitress works for
14 Clump of earth
15 Scent
16 Thought
17 Wildlife area home to red-shouldered hawks in Dunn County (2 wds.)
19 Family group
20 Deadly virus
21 Rapper Dr. ___
22 Detained
23 Tan
26 Cosmonaut Gagarin
28 Wildlife area home to a herd of buffalo in Wood County
32 Heathens
36 Rage
37 Implied
39 "I have ___ up to here!" (2 wds.)
40 East Indian timber tree
42 Ceased raining (2 wds.)
44 Sneaker brand name
45 To strip of equipment
47 Frenchmen Descartes and Coty
49 Long time
50 Philosopher Blaise
52 Wildlife Area home to rare plants in Marinette County

54 Chicken dish
56 ___ Runnings
57 Swedish musical group
60 Cry for help (abbr.)
62 Mountain and National Forest in Utah
66 Pounce
67 Wildlife Area home to black bears in Sawyer County
70 Group of three
71 Peaceful race in The Time Machine
72 Poet Lazarus
73 Beetle Bailey dog
74 Neck parts
75 Witnessed

Down

1 Brand for Wile E. Coyote
2 Word after golf or night
3 Type of list (2 wds.)
4 Confused
5 Tic ___ Toe
6 Hockey great Bobby
7 ___ the line (behaved)
8 Nail file board
9 Cosmetics
10 Wildlife Area home to sandhill cranes and Blanding's turtles in Racine County
11 Not active
12 Ring

13 Box filler
18 Pricey boat
24 Money in Iran
25 Stomach lesion
27 Cheer
28 Abdominal exercise (hyph.)
29 Sports stadium
30 Gets closer
31 Ad ___ (appointed guardian)
33 "I bid you ___"
34 Camera manufacturer
35 Office worker
38 Loose-fitting cloak
41 ___ River Wildlife Area home to great egrets in Crawford County
43 Mexican money
46 Moo goo ___ pan
48 Scrub
51 Abate
53 Dress styles
55 Ta da!
57 Singing voice
58 Ernie's pal
59 Fisherman's need
61 Pig feed
63 Title
64 Clock's reading
65 Actor Alda
68 Compete
69 Winding curve

Solution on page 141.

All the words below are names of state wildlife areas in Wisconsin. The words are encrypted in the same code. Can you break the code to read the names of all the state wildlife areas? As a solving aid, the words are listed in alphabetical order. For an extra hint, see the bottom of the page.

1 RFZWJUXRF ZYKHVLZ

2 EJHYRL ZWRWQKT

3 MYKPJU PRYYJN

4 MUJS FJRXKAZ

5 JRH VRYYJ UQPJU

6 DUJTML MUJJC

7 VRUXTJU ZARFI

8 LKUQMKT FRUZL

9 CQYYZTRCJ

10 CQFEJUYN MYRUC

11 YRCJ TKBHJERN

12 TJA FHTZWJU

13 TKUWL EJTX EKWWKFZ

14 IQTJ QZYRTX

15 UKFJ IKTX

16 ZMHIIJUTKTV

17 WKF YRAQT

18 WKWRVRWQM YRCJ

19 ARWJUYKK

20 ALQWFRT XRF

Hint: Number ten is also the name of a paper company founded in Neenah.

Solution on page 141.

All the words below are names of state trails in Wisconsin. The words are encrypted in the same code. Can you break the code to read the names of all the state trails? As a solving aid, the words are listed in alphabetical order. For an extra hint, see the bottom of the page.

1 JKBJCPP

2 ZJIQPD

3 ZPJDUNGB

4 ZOMMJAY DGEPD

5 FJCGXJA FGXW

6 FJXXJGA

7 PGUPBZJKB

8 MYT DGEPD

9 QJBIW IJBFPD

10 QAJFGJA IDORAGB

11 QDPPB DGEPD

12 RGAGXJDW DGIQP

13 RYOBXJGB-ZJW

14 YAI JZP

15 DPI FPIJD

16 UJOBIPDU

17 XYRYDDYH DGEPD

18 XOUFYZGJ

19 HGAI QYYUP

20 HGYOHJUK

Hint: Number two is also the state animal

Solution on page 141.

Wisconsin Environmental Quote Game

To read the following three quotes about Wisconsin and the environment, you must first solve the clues below. Put the answer on the blanks and then transfer the letters into the grid above according to the number under its blank. Work back and forth to solve.

1I	2K	■	3F	4G	5J	6E	■	7D	8I	9B	10N	11E	12C	13K	14H	■	15L	16D	17P
18I	19M	20J	21G	22B	23E	■	24O	25E	26B	27C	28A	29H	30D	31L	32G	33Q	■	34O	35F
36E	37B	38H	39Q	40D	41I	42M	43C	■	44E	45I	46B	■	47M	48C	49I	■	50A	51P	52O
53H	■	54N	55I	■	56J	57L	58H	■	59N	60H	61A	62K	■	63O	64K	65B	66E	67N	■
68C	69F	■	70H	71B	72G	■	73D	74B	75L	76J	78M	77K	■	79B	80M	81O	82J	■	83K
84H	85P	86F	87J	88I	89A	■	90B	91G	92F	93L	94A	95E	■	96Q	97N	98C	99M	■	100J
101F	102Q	103A	104D	105G	106C	■	107C	108E	109G	110Q	111F	112N	113D	■	114J	115F	116D	■	117M
118P	119H	120O	121A	122H	123L	124G	125C	126Q	127B	128H	■	129I	130G	131Q	132M	133K	134F	135E	
136G	137J	138P	139M	■	140N	141G	142L	143D	■	144I	145F	146K	■	147B	148G	149I			

— Quote by John Muir

A ___ ___ ___ ___ ___ ___ ___
89 103 121 28 50 94 61
More precipitous

B ___ ___ ___ ___ ___ ___ ___ ___ ___ ___ ___ ___
46 71 22 74 90 9 147 37 79 65 26 127
Nocturnal songbird

C ___ ___ ___ ___ ___ ___ ___ ___ ___
43 98 12 125 48 27 107 68 106
Woodchuck

D ___ ___ ___ ___ ___ ___ ___ ___ ___
143 16 30 116 73 104 7 40 113
It's 20/20

E ___ ___ ___ ___ ___ ___ ___ ___ ___ ___
66 36 44 108 23 135 11 6 25 95
Bacterial disease

F ___ ___ ___ ___ ___ ___ ___ ___ ___ ___
145 134 111 35 101 115 3 69 86 92
Placid

G ___ ___ ___ ___ ___ ___ ___ ___ ___ ___ ___ ___
148 130 32 136 141 105 109 4 124 91 21 72
Electrical goods inventor George

H ___ ___ ___ ___ ___ ___ ___ ___ ___ ___ ___
38 53 119 70 60 122 128 58 84 29 14
The old days

I ___ ___ ___ ___ ___ ___ ___ ___ ___ ___ ___
149 41 18 129 88 8 144 49 45 1 55
Five-cent theater or TV network

J ___ ___ ___ ___ ___ ___ ___ ___ ___
100 87 76 56 5 20 82 137 114
Poetic name for England

K ___ ___ ___ ___ ___ ___ ___ ___
2 13 146 64 62 133 83 77
Going fast

L ___ ___ ___ ___ ___ ___ ___
15 123 142 57 31 75 93
Dries up, like a flower

M ___ ___ ___ ___ ___ ___ ___ ___ ___
132 80 99 78 19 117 139 42 47
Notable events

N ___ ___ ___ ___ ___ ___ ___
59 54 97 140 67 10 112
Watchers

O ___ ___ ___ ___ ___ ___
63 34 24 120 81 52
Tin alloy

P ___ ___ ___ ___ ___
138 51 17 85 118
Like the smell in an attic

Q ___ ___ ___ ___ ___ ___ ___
126 96 102 39 110 131 33
Wide stretches

Solution on page 142.

Wisconsin Environmental Quote Game

1B		2C	3D	4C	5B	6A	7B	8D		9B	10B		11A	12B	13D		14E	15B	16E
17C		18C		19E	20D	21A	22D	23C		24E	25B		26A	27B	28B	29E	30A	31D	

— Quote by Frank Lloyd Wright

A ___ ___ ___ ___ ___   Color symbolizing ecology
   11 30 6 21 26

B ___ ___ ___ ___ ___ ___ ___ ___ ___ ___   Birthday party ___
   5 10 7 9 25 27 28 1 12 15

C ___ ___ ___ ___ ___   Type of club or a Baldwin brother
   2 18 4 23 17

D ___ ___ ___ ___ ___ ___   Prepared an apple for a pie
   20 3 31 22 8 13

E ___ ___ ___ ___ ___   St. ___, Missouri
   16 14 29 24 19

1H	2D		3F	4C	5M	6G		7D	8K		9A	10L	11D	12M		13A	14D		15H
	16C	17M	18E	19B	20A		21G	22I	23J	24C	25B	26A	27D		28J	29I	30E		31F
32M	33G	34A	35H		36K	37H	38G	39D	40B		41C	42F	43I	44M		45J	46D		47F
	48C	49F	50J	51D	52B	53K		54B	55K	56L		57F	58E		59J	60M	61B		62G
63I	64C		65B	66G	67H	68A		69H	70F	71L		72E	73G		74F	75D	76B	77H	78K
	79D	80M	81F	82C	83G	84I	85K	86H	87A	88B	89L		90D	91G		92J	93E		94M	95C
96L		97I	98B	99A		100I	101E	102B	103M	104I	105H		106K	107A	108E		109C	110G
111C	112A	113G	114I															

— Quote by Aldo Leopold

A ___ ___ ___ ___ ___ ___ ___ ___ ___ ___   Treats roughly
   9 13 20 112 87 99 68 107 26 34

B ___ ___ ___ ___ ___ ___ ___ ___ ___ ___ ___   Northwoods city
   88 65 25 61 19 52 98 102 54 76 40

C ___ ___ ___ ___ ___ ___ ___ ___ ___ ___   Acts committed by aliens?
   95 41 16 4 24 111 82 109 64 48

D ___ ___ ___ ___ ___ ___ ___ ___ ___ ___ ___   Tomfoolery
   27 75 90 11 7 46 39 51 79 2 14

E ___ ___ ___ ___ ___ ___ ___   Biological study of animals
   18 58 93 108 72 101 30

F ___ ___ ___ ___ ___ ___ ___ ___   Victorious
   3 42 31 49 70 47 81 74

G ___ ___ ___ ___ ___ ___ ___ ___ ___ ___ ___   Bubbles
   66 73 110 113 33 83 6 91 62 38 21

H ___ ___ ___ ___ ___ ___ ___ ___ ___ ___   Medicine to block pain
   15 57 67 86 35 37 105 77 1 69

I ___ ___ ___ ___ ___ ___ ___ ___ ___   Ambulance worker
   22 29 104 63 114 84 43 100 97

J ___ ___ ___ ___ ___ ___   Egyptian king slain in Trojan War
   59 23 28 92 45 50

K ___ ___ ___ ___ ___ ___ ___   Punches holes in the turf
   106 78 85 55 36 53 8

L ___ ___ ___ ___ ___   Filling
   89 96 71 10 56

M ___ ___ ___ ___ ___ ___ ___ ___ ___   Unknown author
   60 5 17 80 12 94 103 32 44

Solution on page 142.

Across

1 Partial
5 Wisconsin's highest temperature ever was 114°F in Wisconsin Dells on ___ 13, 1936
9 Teeth specialist's abbr.
12 Unholy
13 Eagle's nest
14 Sweetheart
15 City in Italy or Wisconsin
16 Bury seeds
17 Tear down
18 Wisconsin's average ___ is 45 inches a year
20 Ore excavator
21 Stare modifier
22 Bridge
24 Inhabitant
28 Wisconsin's lowest temperature ever was -55°F in ___ on February 2 and 4, 1996
32 Orange hue
33 Polka or Macarena
34 Lamb's mom
35 Certain
36 Identification pin
37 Pizzazz
38 Nice summer?
39 Nick Jr's *Blue's* ___
40 French river

41 Appleton recorded a shocking 90°F ___ in the 1995 heat wave (2 wds.)
43 Like a no-good apple
44 Entranced
45 Moo Goo ___ Pan
46 Record
49 Wisconsin's average ___ is 31 inches a year
54 Garfield's cry
55 *The* ___ (Streep movie)
57 Mixture
58 Actress ___ Rachel Wood
59 Line spoken to audience
60 David Schwimmer role
61 *Green Eggs and Ham* character
62 Wisconsin's wettest month
63 Saved

Down

1 Towel inscription
2 British river
3 Long car
4 Went by plane
5 Peanut butter's partner
6 Russian mountains
7 Artist Maya ___
8 Still
9 College administrator
10 Confuse
11 Litigant

13 Rapidly
14 Seawater
19 ___ *Easy Pieces*
20 Concocted
22 Tunes
23 Purple-red hue
24 Pried
25 Severe
26 Flung
27 Bother
28 Military trainee
29 Struck a match again
30 Cognizant
31 Middle Eastern republic
33 Challenge
36 Radar image
37 *I* ___ *You Babe*
39 Quarry for 20 Across
40 Type of cloth
42 Shrimp-like creature
43 Lift
45 En ___!
46 Iowa town
47 Russian river
48 Linguist Chomsky
49 Destroy
50 Eating implement
51 Soothing balm
52 Speech impediment
53 ABC hit show
55 Fifth pillar of Islam (var.)
56 Big Ten school (abbr.)

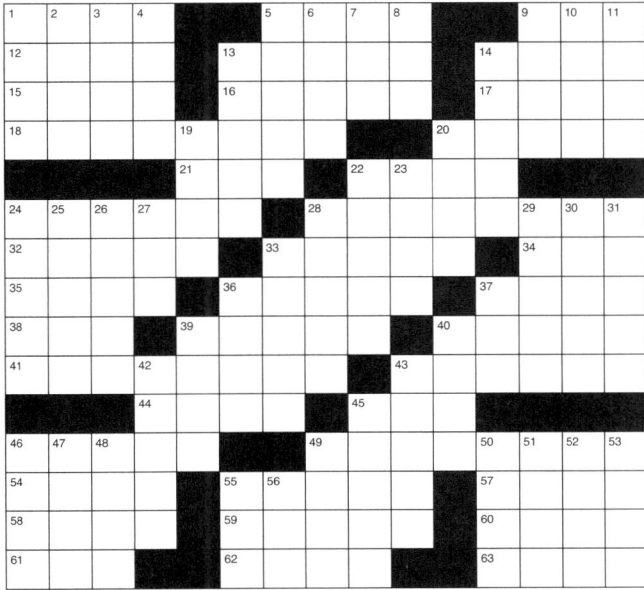

Solution on page 141.

Robin Level

1 What is the coldest month in Wisconsin?

2 What is the driest month in Wisconsin?

3 What is the most active month for tornadoes in Wisconsin?

Musky Level

4 What is the name for the weather phenomenon that can produce heavy snowfall along Wisconsin's north and east borders?

5 In March of 1976, this type of storm became one of the worst natural disasters to hit the state, with 21 counties declared federal disaster areas.

6 The great flooding of the Mississippi River in this year began with heavy rain and flooding of Wisconsin rivers that are tributaries to the Mississippi.

Badger Level

7 The eighth most deadly tornado in the United States, killing 117 people, struck this Wisconsin town on June 12, 1899.

8 The first weather forecast in the nation that was broadcast on radio originated here.

9 A shower of what floated in over Lake Michigan onto eastern Wisconsin in 1881?

 Solution on page 141.

Across

1 Ore mined in SW Wisconsin
5 Author Hoag
9 Hunk of earth
13 Jason's ship
14 *The Phantom of the* ___
16 Wander
17 New Zealand evergreen
18 ___ and crannies
19 Thought
20 What Santa and Abraham Lincoln have in common
22 An F4 tornado hit this Wisconsin town on April 4, 1981
24 Abel's brother
26 Word before date
27 Pasta dish requirement
30 Bon ___ (good price)
35 Mulberries (genus)
36 Light-colored
38 Spoken
39 Related
40 Not now
41 Prison or storm ending
42 Uprising
43 Homeowner's bill (abbr.)
44 It could be ice or roller
45 Grand ___ National Park
47 Little pieces, in Yiddish
49 *Sex and the City's* Mr. ___

51 Therefore
52 An F5 tornado devastated this Wisconsin town on July 18, 1996
57 New
61 Teenager's bane
62 Model Campbell
64 Upper part of a glacier
65 Magnolia or dogwood
66 Pas de ___ (a dance for three)
67 Stumble
68 Cad
69 Son of Shem
70 Dog's cry

Down

1 Spring animal
2 Smallest of the Great Lakes
3 Taj Mahal site
4 An F3 tornado slashed through this Wisconsin tourist area on August 23, 1998 (2 wds.)
5 Oft-removed appendage
6 Soldier's mail collection site (abbr.)
7 Cat's cry
8 Bothered
9 Baby's bed
10 Mother ___ (gold mine)

11 Kitchen appliance
12 Beat a ___ horse
15 Pretender
21 Fathers
23 Afternoon drink
25 Himalayan country
27 Cell phone maker
28 Mythological hunter
29 Quenches
31 An F4 tornado surprised this southern Wisconsin area with a November 11, 1911, strike
32 Floorboard noise
33 Stops
34 Fashion magazine
35 Roman ruler Antony
37 La ___ League
40 Easy-going
44 Type of language
46 Japanese sash
48 Self-evident fact
50 Stand out
52 Promise
53 Plot of land
54 Patella location
55 Sense
56 NBC soap opera (abbr.)
58 Withered
59 Inhuman
60 Actor Johnny
63 Unaccounted for soldier (abbr.)

Solution on page 142.

Tornado Sudoku

Fill all empty squares so that the nine letters appear once in each row, column, and 3x3 box. The answer, reading across the middle row, will reveal the site of the Labor Day Tornado of 2002.

A			T			H		
I				M	D		S	
	H					M	I	
S	T				L			Y
M			D				A	L
	D	S					Y	
	M		A	Y				I
		A			T			S

Across

1 Tree covering
5 West of Nev.
10 Skillful
14 Unknown author (abbr.)
15 Mission San Antonio de Valero
16 Forehead
17 Suffix meaning female
18 Puerto ___, (Rita Moreno, for example)
19 Garden device
20 Falls in the Turtle River, Iron County (2 wds.)
22 Peony or pansy, e.g.
24 Munched
25 Realize
26 Premieres
30 Young salmon
31 Tree juice
34 Waken
35 ___ and dangerous
36 Pair
37 *Splendor in the Grass* playwright William
38 Smooth
39 Apartment type
40 Edge
41 Silenced
42 360 spin in a car
43 Nay opposite
44 ___ for business

45 They're eaten with lox
46 Politician Ralph
48 Infection site for many kids
49 Base coat of paint
51 Falls in Bayfield County near Cornucopia
56 Whit
57 It could be graven
59 Carnival attraction
60 Neighbor of Thailand
61 Vows
62 The aqueduct of Sylvius
63 Ostrich kins
64 Scarlett's sometime adversary
65 Pretense

Down

1 1934 Heavyweight Champion of the World and actor Max
2 Against (prefix)
3 Campus military group
4 Between the tibia and femur
5 Jewel weights
6 Similar
7 Frilly fabric
8 "___ little teapot..."(2 wds.)
9 Falls in Brown County over the Niagara Escarpment
10 Detest
11 30-foot falls in Copper Falls State Park

12 Be defeated
13 Pitcher
21 Tardy
23 Fat
25 Injured
26 Major industry in Wisconsin
27 Bert's buddy
28 At 165 feet, highest falls in Wisconsin (2 wds.)
29 Consume
30 Primp
32 Terrible
33 Actress Annie
35 Change
38 90-foot falls on the Montreal River on border with Michigan
39 ___ jam
41 Fashion
42 Unlit
45 Most vile
47 Stock
48 Magic ___ Ball
49 Lump
50 Wander
51 Stuff
52 Spring bloom
53 Along
54 Light bulb in comics
55 Semester
58 ___ -jongg

Solution on page 142.

```
K C O T N I L C C M N O S P U
I B T W A O E O H S E S R O H
M M U E X R U P C K R E T T L
B A Y L G I M P B Y W I V A D
A D D V L E T E R G N O R T S
L S N E E N A R F A N L O O P
L Y U F D T C O M S A U C R R
A A G O X A E E N A G T K I I
S H H O R S L R I X R O C V N
A S G T E T Y G A O O S U E G
L E U G T N O C I N M A T R C
L V O I S P E T E R S O N I A
E A L L O N G S L I D E R V M
S D S E F E G R O G S R E I P
```

Find the names (capitalized words only) of the Wisconsin waterfalls in the grid above.

AMNICON Falls

BULL Falls

COPPER Falls

DAVE'S Falls

FOSTER Falls

GILE Falls

HORSESHOE Falls

KIMBALL Falls

LA SALLE Falls

LITTLE MANITOU Falls

LONG SLIDE Falls

MCCLINTOCK Falls

MORGAN Falls

ORIENTA Falls

PETERSON Falls

PIERS GORGE Falls

POTATO RIVER Falls

ROCK CUT Falls

SAXON Falls

SHAYS DAM Falls

SLOUGH GUNDY Falls

SPRING CAMP Falls

STRONG Falls

TWELVE FOOT Falls

UPSON Falls

VETERANS Falls

WREN Fall

Solution on page 148.

Wisconsin Lighthouses

Across
1 Win, place, or ___
5 Intended
10 Sense
14 ___ cleaner
15 Curve in a stream
16 Recent
17 Toward shelter
18 San ___, CA
19 Taj Mahal city
20 Private lighthouse on Lake Winnebago, Oshkosh
22 Scolded
24 Beer
25 English metric unit
26 Clans
30 ___ the way (prepare)
31 Underwear trademark
34 Talon
35 Actor Beatty
37 Falsehood
38 ___ time (2 wds.)
39 ___ *Time* by Ernest Hemingway (2 wds.)
40 Speechless
41 Mauna ___
42 Some garden statues
43 Distant
44 Black tropical cuckoo
45 "What are the ___?"
46 Ransack (with through)
47 Gradient
49 Misery

51 Franklin Roosevelt's middle name
53 Apostle Island lighthouse
58 "___ poor Yorick!"
59 Incensed
61 Singer Celine
62 Money-making site
63 38 across synonym
64 Margarine
65 Football player's needs
66 Crown
67 Fewer

Down
1 Box
2 Big Island city
3 Oil group (abbr.)
4 Calendar unit
5 Pose
6 Deport
7 First murder victim
8 Egg ___
9 Lighthouse that's part of Historic Rogers Street Fishing Village Museum in Manitowoc County (2 wds.)
10 Panache
11 Lighthouse in Peninsula State Park (2 wds.)
12 To be (Fr.)
13 Ore mined in SE Wisconsin
21 Used to be

23 Group of asteroids
25 Demi and Bruce's daughter Scout ___ Willis
26 Milan opera house "La ___"
27 Musician John
28 Lighthouse on east side of Door County (2 wds.)
29 Duo
30 High school balls
32 Essential
33 Last name in tractors
35 Oldest and tallest Great Lakes lighthouse in Racine (2 wds.)
36 Electrode
40 ___ tai cocktail
42 Thug
46 Motorcar company of early 1900s
48 Remains
49 *Like ___ for Chocolate*
50 Landmark Sydney ___ House
51 Dank
52 Famous essayist
53 Mount Vesuvius output
54 *American ___*
55 River in Africa
56 Foot appendages
57 Fourth book of Mormon
60 Outdoor gear store

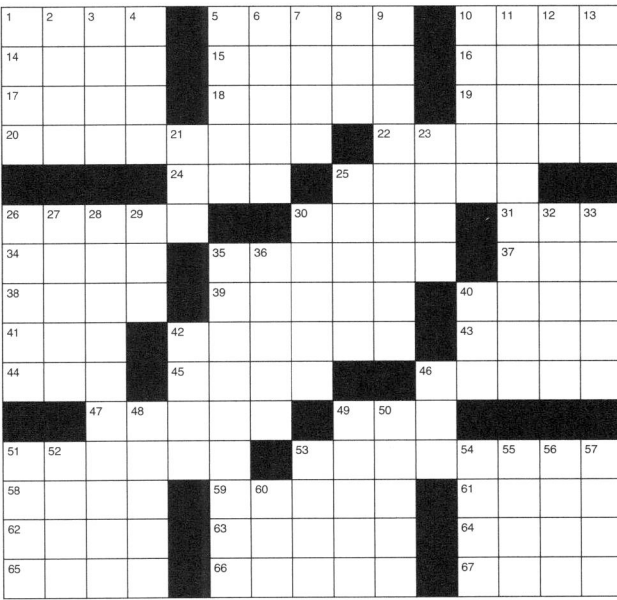

Solution on page 142.

73

More Wisconsin Lighthouses

Find the names (capitalized words only) of the Wisconsin lighthouses in the accompanying grid.

ALGOMA	MILWAUKEE Breakwater
ASHLAND Breakwater	NEENAH
ASYLUM Point	NORTH Point
BAILEYS HARBOR	OUTER Island
BOYER BLUFF	PESHTIGO REEF
BRAYS Point	PILOT Island
CHAMBERS Island	PLUM Island
CHEQUAMEGON Point	PORT WASHINGTON
DEVILS Island	POTTAWATOMIE
FISHERMAN'S ROAD	RACINE Harbor
FOND DU LAC	RASPBERRY Island
GOVERNMENT	RAWLEY Point
GRASSY ISLAND RANGE	ROCK Island
GREEN Island	SAND Island
GULL Island	SHEBOYGAN Breakwater
KENOSHA	SHERWOOD Point
KEWAUNEE Pier	STURGEON BAY
LONG TAIL Point	CANAL STATION
MANITOWOC Breakwater	WISCONSIN Point
MICHIGAN Island	

```
S H E B O Y G A N O G E M A U Q E H C N
R L R O E N A G I H C I M R C M U S O O
E A S Y L U M A N I T W E N I G H T W I
B R G E R A C I N E O T A Y S E I G O T
M S O R C G H M A D U B N L R A B R T A
A L D B A N I S N O C S I W Y S R W I T
H F N L I S B A R N L V O C E Q A O N S
C H A U N O S V E A E O N H L U Y O A L
N O L F G L L Y H D D C S I W A S P M A
F D H F O V B A I L E Y S H A R B O R N
F I S H E R M A N S R O A D R A W R O A
O R A S T E L H M I L W A U K E E T N C
N C A U T W R E E W Y A R E C A L W D Y
D K Q S O I Y O F H K M N E I S I A U A
D R O F P C U A G N T O L D V T A S K B
U H Y L U B M K E I S R P A R O T H E N
L F U L B O E D L H T I O G S A G I W O
A M S L G W A R A B K H A N E E N N A E
C W A L A K B T R C R T S N G T O G N G
H R A U S P N E O Y P O U E E I L T E R
F I N G O V E R N M E N T C P E N O N U
R E K W E M O S P O R L N I A L R N O T
E I M O T A W A T T O P I L O T A G L S
```

Solution on page 148.

Apostle Islands

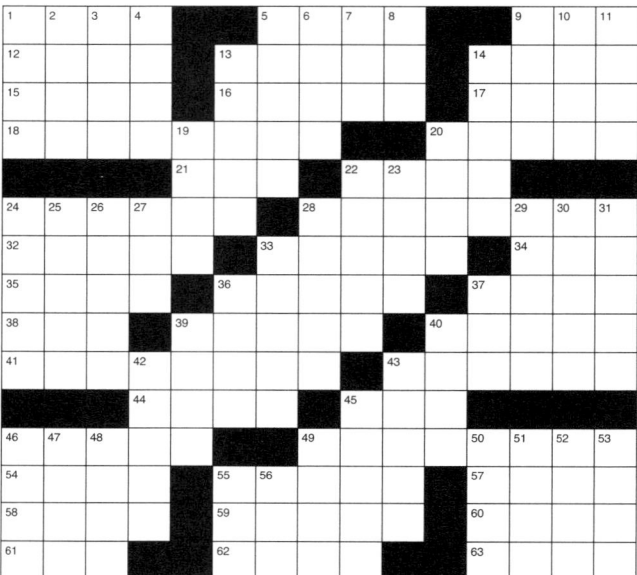

Across

1 Exchange blows
5 Collegiate sport
9 What an athlete will do in 5 Across
12 Kilauea's product
13 Designer Ashley
14 Gambling town
15 Bothers
16 Frosting
17 Paradise
18 Apostle Island known to the Ojibwe as "Hook and Line Island"
20 Hog sound
21 Greek letter
22 "Get ___ to a nunnery"
24 Apostle Island known to the Ojibwe as "The Further Island"
28 Apostle Island noted on an 1871 map as "Higgins Island"
32 He was at ___ for words (2 wds.)
33 Bore the ___ of
34 After JKL
35 Drugs, briefly
36 Quench
37 Some Scots
38 Type of bandage
39 Turnpike rest stop
40 Varying pitch
41 Apostle Island known to the Ojibwe as "Almost an Island"
43 Apostle Island known to the Ojibwe as "Evil Spirit Island"
44 Its capital is Tehran
45 POW-___
46 Bear native to China
49 Apostle Island also known as "Isle Michel"
54 Fencing sword
55 Saint's belonging
57 Cast ___ (Tom Hanks movie)
58 Shakespearean King
59 Something to remember
60 Extensive
61 Flub
62 Call ___ on something (stake a claim)
63 Famous Scottish lake

Down

1 Thin
2 Prefix meaning equal
3 With (Fr.)
4 Foolhardy
5 Chocolate tree
6 Destroy
7 Sea eagle
8 Tail movement
9 Make over
10 Doozy
11 "This ___ hurt a bit"
13 Like a feather
14 Library activity
19 Spring bloom
20 Heaven ___
22 Bind
23 Sharpen
24 Militant Islamic group
25 Choose
26 Cowboy's tournament
27 Documents (abbr.)
28 Golfer Hale
29 Muscat native
30 Actress Tatum
31 Girls' toys
33 Nucleus with an even mass number
36 Info
37 State leader, briefly
39 Gumbo ingredient
40 Green and black, for example
42 Apple beverage
43 70s dance craze
45 Injures
46 Hawaiian volcano goddess
47 Imitator
48 Close
49 Rat
50 Alert
51 Boo-boo
52 Dolts
53 Colors
55 Slang for cool
56 Inventor Whitney

Solution on page 142.

Robin Level

1 Which Wisconsin city is the gateway to the Apostle Islands?

2 A large group of islands such as the Apostle Islands is known as what?

3 Which island did the Native Americans say was the home of Matchimanitou, the "evil spirit"?

Musky Level

4 In 2004, 80% of the Apostle Islands National Lakeshore became a federally protected wilderness area named after which Wisconsin governor and senator?

5 What is the name of the largest Apostle Island, which is not part of the national lakeshore?

6 Scuba divers at Apostle Island National Lakeshore tour what attractions named *Lucerne*, *Noquebay*, *Sevona*, and *Pretoria*?

Badger Level

7 In what era was the sandstone deposited that makes up the renowned cliff formations?

8 Climate change has been blamed for what record lows recently in the Apostle Islands?

9 Stockton Island and Presque Isle are an excellent example of land connected by a narrow sand deposit. What is the term for that kind of landform?

Solution on page 142. **77**

Apostle Island Facts

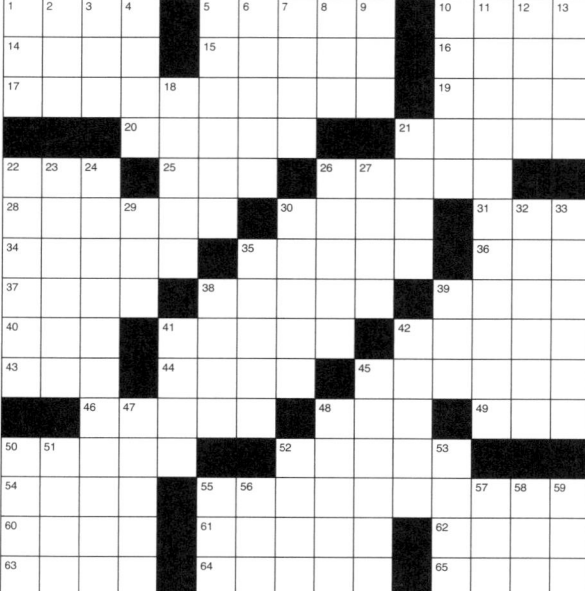

Across

1 Stretches the truth
5 Lover
10 Tag words on damaged clothing
14 Emollient
15 Siskel's former partner
16 Crooked
17 Stockton Island has the world's greatest concentration of ___ (2 wds.)
19 Like a doily
20 Browned bread
21 Calm down
22 Triages
25 ___ 66
26 ___ Ingalls Wilder
28 Native American tent
30 Heap
31 Store owner with Pop
34 Nurse Barton
35 Beeped
36 New homeowner's fee (abbr.)
37 Take a walk in the woods
38 Back ___ Future (2 wds.)
39 Mars's Greek name
40 NASA's cousin abroad
41 Like some towelettes
42 Stone monument with carvings
43 Timid
44 ___ meeny miny moe
45 The ___, Tim Robbins movie

46 Dread
48 Lady's garment
49 Pig's home
50 Makes cookies
52 Condemns
54 Part of the eye
55 Most important quarry in Apostle Islands in the past
60 Time of fasting
61 Darkened
62 Inappropriately MIA
63 Falls behind
64 San ___, CA
65 Ruby and scarlet

Down

1 Da bomb
2 Sick
3 Feather scarf
4 Division
5 Refund
6 Portly
7 ___ loaf
8 Flub
9 Extra innings
10 More physically competent
11 Invasion of ___ cut the fishing industry in the Apostle Islands (2 wds.)
12 Quechuan group member
13 River in Hades
18 Divided land

21 Regretted
22 Carves
23 Hot dog topping
24 Popular sport in the Apostle Islands (2 wds.)
26 Six historic ___ stations in the Apostle Islands are the largest group in any unit of the national park system
27 Toward the sheltered side
29 Ante synonym
30 Sucker
32 Breakfast dish
33 Stephen King movie
35 The Apostle Islands is Wisconsin's northernmost ___
38 On tippy ___
39 Be ___ loss (2 wds.)
41 Ryan and Tilly
42 Hits
45 Right away
47 Prepares for a baby
48 British singer David
50 Unwelcome mail
51 Length times width
52 Blockhead
53 Sirius or Polaris
55 Freeloader
56 Messenger nucleotides
57 Write an IOU
58 Sway like a flower
59 Chicago trains

Solution on page 143.

HISTORY & GOVERNMENT

Evidence of humans in Wisconsin has been found dating back 6,000 years in places such as Copper Culture State Park and the Durst Rockshelter in Sauk County. Many groups of Native Americans called this land home over the past thousand years, and some of them still do.

Europeans came to the area starting in 1634. Both France and Great Britain lay claim to the land before it became a United States territory in 1836. Early government dealt with issues of slavery and temperance and the location for the capitol, which eventually found its way to the city between the lakes. Wisconsin has had its proud moments in politics, as with the La Follette years and the formation of the Progressive Party, and its not-so-proud moments, as with Joseph McCarthy and the Red Scare.

Wisconsin has done a good job in preserving historical sites and commemorating its past. We have much to pay tribute to, with many "firsts" occurring here and many ingenious innovations. But we have also had our dark days when war, fire, and tragedy have tested our perseverance. As the adage says, "Those who do not learn from history are doomed to repeat it."

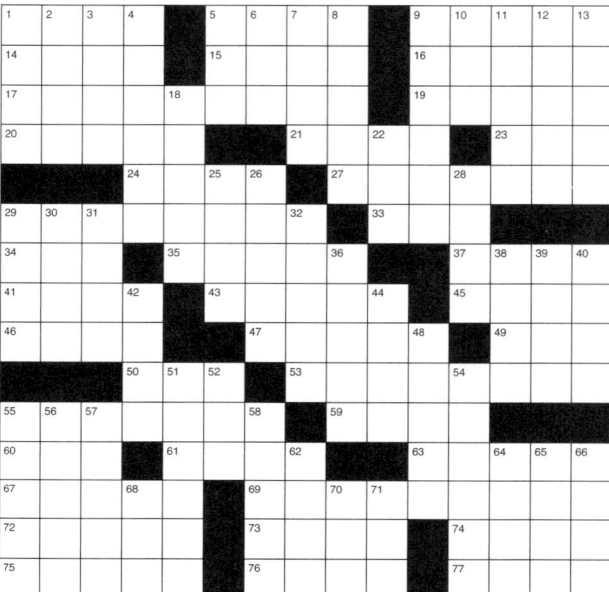

Across

1 Actresses Vardalos and Peeples
5 Column in addition
9 Hurried
14 Smallest Great Lake
15 Berserk
16 Love
17 Civil-War era historic stage coach inn in Greenbush (2 wds.)
19 Earn
20 Pester
21 Some sheep
23 Hole-in-one
24 Zone
27 Astral
29 ___ Wisconsin, 65 buildings of pioneer times and ethnic culture displays in Eagle (2 wds.)
33 Do ___ say... (2 wds.)
34 Author Edgar Allan
35 Extinct birds
37 Speak with a grating voice
41 Fencer's sword
43 Plasma
45 Sore
46 Dweeb
47 Singer LeAnn
49 ___ the cows come home
50 Wane

53 ___ Museum, 1890s lumber company farm and steam train in Laona (2 wds.)
55 Fragrant, late spring bloomers
59 Spiral
60 Type of investor (abbr.)
61 Horse for breeding
63 Your sister's daughter
67 Clumsy
69 Early 1800s Cornish stone cottages from lead mining heyday in Mineral Point
72 Stair part
73 Race in *The Time Machine*
74 Green and camomile
75 Take care of (2 wds.)
76 Peel
77 ___ gin fizz

Down

1 Salamander
2 *Dies* ___ (Latin hymn)
3 Verdi opera
4 Teeter-totter
5 Ultimate principle of the universe
6 Flightless bird
7 What a horse might win by
8 Slants
9 Great Pharaoh ___ II
10 Diluted fruit juice

11 ___ reef
12 Writer Jong
13 Dissuade
18 Ancient king of Judea
22 Airport stat.
25 God of Love
26 Type of tree
28 Turkish money
29 ___ for business
30 Gait
31 Like a ___ in the headlights
32 Type of Greek architecture
36 Bright red autumn shrub/tree
38 Play opener (2 wds.)
39 Makeshift knife
40 Hawaiian goddess
42 Utopia
44 Note
48 ___ bifida
51 Cafe
52 Wager
54 Acts playfully
55 Duos
56 Golfer Els
57 Fat
58 Wonderful
62 Lunch counter
64 Daredevil Knievel
65 Italian greeting
66 To be (Latin)
68 House cat
70 ___ sequitur
71 *I Know What You* ___ *Last Summer*

Solution on page 143.

Robin Level

1 Wisconsin was the ___ state admitted to the union.

2 Why is southwestern Wisconsin called the driftless region?

3 This major city was once three separate villages named Juneautown, Kilbourntown, and Walker's Point.

Musky Level

4 Wisconsin was the first state in the nation to ratify the Nineteenth Amendment, which did what?

5 What was the nickname for Wisconsin miners who made their homes in caves or dug-outs?

6 What was Wisconsin's first export?

Badger Level

7 During World War II, what group of people was housed at Camp McCoy and did agricultural work there?

8 Which former president was shot in front of Milwaukee's Hotel Gilpatrick in 1912?

9 When Jean Nicolet first landed in Wisconsin near Green Bay, where did he think he was?

Solution on page 142.

Explorers in Wisconsin

Across

1 Releases
6 Hidden holiday items
10 Vessels for the covenant and Noah
14 Major artery
15 Yuletide
16 Smallest of the pack
17 To Catch a ___
18 International money
19 Cookie used in piecrusts
20 Vacillate
22 Label
23 MN's ___ of America
24 17th Greek letter
26 Explorer who visited Wisconsin lands along Lake Michigan in the late 1600s
28 Marquette's 1673 partner in traversing WI's rivers to the Mississippi
32 Crime scene clue
33 East of Europe
34 Dined
36 Flip-flop
41 Negative qualities
42 Frog's cousins
45 Copycat
46 Carefree
48 Urban music style
49 Heavenly in Hawaiian
50 Chicken ___ King (2 wds.)
53 French fur trader and first European in WI in 1634

55 Missionary priest who visited WI from 1665-1670
59 Snakelike marine life
60 Ray
61 Chat
63 Forest inhabitant (var.)
68 Make cookies
69 Zeal
71 Bread
72 Place for 68 Across
73 AKA Lucius Domitius Ahenobarbus
74 Actor Dennehey
75 Guarding ___
76 Shucks
77 Solar system body discovered in 2003

Down

1 Singer Domino
2 Architect Mies van der ___
3 Great Lake
4 Riviera summers
5 African excursion
6 Direction of the Apostle Islands from Superior
7 Arthritic condition
8 President Ford
9 Motto
10 Smell
11 Out of town
12 Funeral bell
13 Fur wrap

21 WI was the leading producer of ___ in 1840s
25 Prince von Bismarck
27 Before Sun.
28 Clink
29 Formerly Christiania
30 Stitch's partner
31 Young girl
35 Word before canal
37 Angel accoutrement
38 October birthstone
39 State Bird of Hawaii
40 True ___
43 Madison's county
44 Eavesdrops
47 ___ Claire
51 Lombardi, for example
52 Ornamental shrub
54 Hikes upward
55 Monks' superior
56 Vacate
57 WI has 15,081 of them
58 Portents
62 Rural structure
64 Word after folk
65 Vacuum
66 Singer Jackson
67 Grandma
70 Christmas drink

Solution on page 143.

Great Dates

The following are memorable moments in Wisconsin history. Can you match the notable event to the year in which it happened?

A 1661

B 1673

C 1764

D 1818

E 1832

F 1836

G 1848

H 1851

I 1871

J 1900

K 1904

L 1919

M 1934

N 1959

O 1970

P 1979

Q 1993

R 2001

1 First state fair

2 State capitol burns

3 Circus World Museum established in Baraboo

4 Father Rene Menard becomes first missionary in Wisconsin

5 Peshtigo Fire

6 18th Amendment (Prohibition) ratified

7 Green Bay becomes first permanent settlement in Wisconsin

8 Cryptosporidium outbreak in Milwaukee

9 Black Hawk War

10 First state park created

11 Wisconsin becomes a state

12 Marquette and Jolliet paddle the Wisconsin River and reach the Mississippi River

13 Sterling Hall bombed

14 Solomon Juneau begins a trading post at what will become Milwaukee

15 Chronic Wasting Disease is discovered in Wisconsin

16 Territory of Wisconsin is created

17 First woman is elected to Wisconsin's Supreme Court

18 Progressive Party formed

Solution on page 143.

Wisconsin Inventors

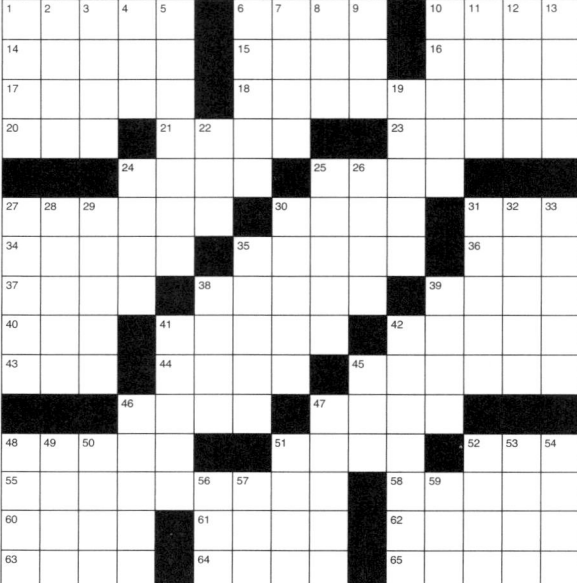

Across

1 Hypothesize
6 Cleaning agent
10 Who, ___, when, ___, and ___
(with 10 Down and 45 Down)
14 Jazz singer O'Day
15 Major or Minor starter
16 Adios's opposite
17 Say
18 Gottfried ___ of Milwaukee
made the first gasoline-
powered tractor in 1886
20 ___ Alamo, NM
21 Tee hee
23 Arbor plants
24 Partial
25 Seeger or Sampras
27 In 1903 in Milwaukee,
Arthur Davidson and William
___ invented a one-cylinder
motorcycle
30 I'll ___ your word for it
31 Faint
34 Perfect
35 Stiff
36 Mother of the ancient
Irish gods
37 "___ have a cow"
38 Stiff
39 Wisconsin grilling food
40 Hitherto
41 Showy fall shrub
42 Parisian river

43 Make your own clothes
44 Wading bird
45 Charles H. ___ of Beloit invented the auto speedometer
46 Worry
47 Avoid
48 Row
51 Simon ___
52 Part of a circle
55 UW professor Harry ___
invented a cure for rickets
58 Sailing (2 wds.)
60 Pimples
61 African medical plant
62 Billionaire Bill
63 Advanced degrees (abbr.)
64 Word ___ around...
65 School in Paris

Down

1 Les ___ of Waukesha in-
vented the electric guitar
2 Atop
3 Rests
4 Wisconsin ending
5 North Carolinian (2 wds.)
6 Japanese dish
7 Predatory whale
8 Falls from volcanoes
9 Buddy
10 See 10 Across
11 Residence
12 Downwind

13 ___ and feathers
19 Swimming mammal
22 Singer Grant
24 Thin strip of wood
25 Kind of button
26 ___ out a living
27 Cowers
28 Love
29 Freshen
30 Frat party garments
31 Teen idol Bobby
32 Nuts
33 Alma ___
35 Word on a highway sign
38 ___ Goldberg device
39 Capital of Switzerland
41 Fire whistle
42 Races at Miller Park
45 See 10 Across
46 Instead of fights
47 For goodness ___
48 Right now
49 Scratch
50 Mail
51 Great ___!
52 Regarding (2 wds.)
53 Cinema device
54 J.I. ___ invented a treadmill-
powered threshing and
separating machine in 1849
56 Sack
57 Bull ring cheer
59 Tic ___ toe

Solution on page 143.

Robin Level

1 Name the two most infamous killers who lived in Wisconsin.

2 The worst forest fire in the nation killed 1,200 people around this city in 1871.

3 This UW-Madison building was shattered and one person was killed by a car bomb placed by antiwar radicals in 1970.

Musky Level

4 Chai Soua Vang shot and killed six members of this type of party in northwest Wisconsin in November 2004.

5 The construction crane dubbed "Big Blue" collapsed in a high wind, killing three workers during the building of this structure in 1999.

6 What triggered Wisconsin's deadliest multiple car accident, taking 10 lives on I-43 in October 2003?

Badger Level

7 Strikes over this Wisconsin product in the 1930s resulted in the bombing of seven factories.

8 In 1860, the *Lady Elgin*, a steamboat that was carrying Milwaukee residents back from an outing in Chicago, sank after colliding with this. About 300 people aboard the *Lady Elgin* drowned.

9 James R. Vineyard shot and killed C.C. Arndt in 1842 in this public location.

Solution on page 143.

Wisconsin's Oldest

Across

1 Coffeehouse
5 Mountain ridge
10 Female horse
14 *Yours, Mine, and* ___
15 Boston airport name
16 Surrounded by
17 Valuable rocks
18 The Potawatomi ___ on Washington Island is the oldest in Wisconsin
20 Coating
22 Aching
23 Kohl, for example (abbr.)
24 Highbrows
27 Widest shoe size
28 Road curve
29 Gazelle
32 Yale student
34 Afternoon drink
35 Merits
37 Criticize
41 Scraps
43 ___ Ste. Marie
45 Barge
46 Ford ___ Company
48 Attempted
50 Compass point
51 Yang's counterpart
53 May birthstones
55 ___ Vegas

58 Singer Morrison
60 B-29 ___ *Gay*
61 Constellation of the Altar
62 British school
64 Mugs in a pub
67 Wisconsin's oldest ___ is a Greek Revival design in Iowa County built in 1861
71 Fix the text
72 Italian noble family
73 Actor Ed from *Lou Grant*
74 Number on a baseball team
75 Spore
76 Retreats
77 Bamboozle

Down

1 ___ *Hand Luke*
2 Radiant light
3 Wisconsin's oldest German settlement, a word that means "free place"
4 Ancient Jewish sect
5 Free for ___
6 Louis XIV
7 Breakfast choice
8 Nevada lake
9 Main course
10 ___ Zedong
11 Entertain
12 Goes up

13 Utopias
19 Head over ___
21 ___ playing
25 Pythons
26 "Jack ___ could eat no fat"
29 Particle
30 Roman fiddler?
31 Harden
33 ___ and outs
36 Goo
38 Washington Island in Wisconsin is the oldest ___ community in the United States
39 Small lake
40 Mother sheep
42 Bean with a lot of protein
44 Preadult
47 Stud
49 Let go
52 Actor Lane
54 Martians
55 Ties
56 Woke up
57 Panfry
59 Hangman's knot
63 Holy women
65 Actress Fey
66 ___ cell research
68 Cut through the ___ tape
69 Arrange
70 Where ambulances go

Solution on page 144.

Robin Level

1 Name Wisconsin's state bird.

2 Name Wisconsin's state dance.

3 Name Wisconsin's state song.

Musky Level

4 Name Wisconsin's state tree.

5 Name Wisconsin's state motto.

6 Name Wisconsin's state flower.

Badger Level

7 Name Wisconsin's state mineral.

8 Name Wisconsin's state soil.

9 Name Wisconsin's state fossil.

Solution on page 143.

All the words below are items that can be found on the Great Seal of Wisconsin. The words are encrypted in the same code. Can you break the code to read the names of all the items? As a solving aid, the words are listed in alphabetical order. For an extra hint, see the bottom of the page.

1 XEFSTY

2 XYP XEI SXPPWY

3 QXINWY

4 QXYA TB GWXI

5 FTKG TB YTVW

6 FTYEJFTVKX

7 W VGJYKQJA JEJP

8 BTYOXYI

9 PKEWY

10 VKFU XEI ASTDWG

11 VGTO

12 AXKGTY

13 ASKWGI

14 ZSKYZWWE AZXYA

Hint: Number three is an animal.

Solution on page 143.

Robin Level

1 The birth of what special animal in Janesville was regarded as a spiritual sign to many Native Americans around the country?

2 What controversial Native American activity led to riots and "Wisconsin's Walleye War" in the late '80s?

3 This city's name comes from the Native American word "Mahnawaukee-Seepe," meaning gathering place by the river.

Musky Level

4 Which Native American tribe has been active in Wisconsin Dells tourism from the early years on?

5 Name one of the two future US Presidents who fought in Wisconsin during the Black Hawk War.

6 What is the largest Indian Reservation in Wisconsin?

Badger Level

7 Waswagoning, a historical Native American village preserved in Lac de Flambeau, represents what tribe?

8 An intaglio is a burial mound that is cut into the ground. The Panther Intaglio, the last known intaglio remaining in the state, is found in this city.

9 Name the famous Ho-Chunk Indian chief who helped Americans in the Black Hawk War but was then forced out of the state.

Solution on page 143.   **91**

Wisconsin Public Indian Mounds

Across

1 With ready and willing
5 Aromatic spring bloom
10 Model home
14 Lure
15 ___ Colonies in Iowa
16 Not on land
17 Per
18 Ill will
19 Milwaukee's Historic Third ___
20 "To sleep, perchance to ___"
22 Flying ___
24 Recline
25 Little boys
28 6 Indian mounds lie in ___ County Park, overlooking Lake Winnebago
30 12 mounds dating to after 500 AD lie in Indian Mounds Park in ___ (2 wds.)
34 Cellar rodent
35 Wisconsin tree killer, the Emerald ___ Borer
36 Levels
38 Horicon ___
42 Awkward person
44 Perspire
46 Hawaiian city
47 Presidential candidate Alan ___
49 Leftover
51 Tic ___ Toe
52 Munched

54 Indian Mounds Campground in Northern Highlands/ American Legion State Forest near Lake ___
56 The ___ Mound Group can be visited just off Hwy Y in Sauk City
60 Dry
61 Large primate
62 The game was a ___ biter
64 Defunct
68 Plant attacked by 35 Across
70 Unpromising
73 Fool
74 Orient
75 Animal that spits
76 College course (abbr.)
77 New York stadium
78 Composition
79 Family rooms

Down

1 Scored a hole-in-one
2 Wild hog
3 Wedding gown material
4 Breathe out
5 ___ Cruces, NM
6 Rascal
7 Placed
8 Caper
9 Salad dressing name
10 After hand or chain
11 Sacred hymn

12 Spooky
13 Military student
21 Ice cream treat
23 Mollusk
26 Soapbox
27 Slants
29 Provo's state
30 Antlers
31 Small body of land
32 Bok ___
33 Build
37 Gulf of ___ on the Aegean Sea
39 Actress Hayworth
40 Shredded cabbage
41 Pawn
43 Donna Shalala was once UW-Madison's ___
45 Domesticated
48 Amaze
50 Brunet Island State ___
53 Permit
55 Led
56 Abhors
57 Talk show host
58 Actress Witherspoon
59 Fish's breathing organs
63 Meadows
65 Reddish purple
66 On top
67 Hamiltons
69 Truax Field abbreviation
71 US doctor group (abbr.)
72 Mary ___ cosmetics

Solution on page 144.

Fill all empty squares so that the nine letters appear once in each row, column, and 3x3 box. The answer, reading across the middle row, will reveal a tribe driven west into Wisconsin by competing tribes.

				U			C	
S	U		E				M	O
O		A		S				T
C	T		A		N	M	O	
	O	E	S		T		A	U
A				N		U		C
T	M				C		S	E
	E			T				

Solution on page 138.

Chief Black Hawk Quote Game

Put the answer to each clue on the numbered blank. Then transfer the letters into their appropriately numbered spots in the grid above. Work back and forth to solve. When complete, the puzzle will reveal a quote by Sauk Chief Black Hawk.

1I	2J	3L	4D		5E	6H	7A	8E	9G		10K	11D	12B		13C	14I	15B	16E	17D	18B	19F	20G	21A
	22D	23K	24C	25A	26J	27L	28I		29A	30B	31E	32B	33F	34D		35I	36L		37C	38L	39A	40B
41F		42J	43C		44G	45F	46A	47D	48H	49L	50F	51G	52K	53D		54J	55B	56G		57E	58L	59J
60F	61G	62I	63B		64E	65C		66H	67B		68E	69G	70A	71B	72C	73L		74F	75C		76G	77L
78H	79I	80F	81C	82G		83B	84H	85F		86D	87A	88C	89L		90D	91L		92B	93G		94K	95A
96H	97K	98E																				

A _ _ _ _ _ _ _ _ _
39 70 21 7 95 46 29 25 87

Animal mascot from *Red Dawn*

B _ _ _ _ _ _ _ _ _ _ _
71 63 83 55 12 67 30 32 92 40 18 15

Avenue for the White House

C _ _ _ _ _ _ _ _ _
13 24 37 75 88 81 65 72 43

Monarch or Karner Blue

D _ _ _ _ _ _ _ _ _
4 90 22 86 53 17 11 47 34

Prop for a bike

E _ _ _ _ _ _ _ _
16 68 5 31 64 57 8 98

Transplanted

F _ _ _ _ _ _ _ _ _
60 45 80 41 50 85 74 19 33

Like Susan, Bree, or Lynette

G _ _ _ _ _ _ _ _ _ _
56 76 93 44 51 61 82 20 9 69

Full ___ (reveal all)

H _ _ _ _ _ _
66 84 96 6 48 78

Change

I _ _ _ _ _ _
35 14 62 79 1 28

Card matching game

J _ _ _ _ _
42 54 26 59 2

San ___, California

K _ _ _ _ _
10 97 52 23 94

Black ___ spider

L _ _ _ _ _ _ _ _ _ _
58 36 89 38 3 27 49 91 73 77

What they do is not what they say

Solution on page 143.

All the words below are names of past and present Indian tribes in Wisconsin. The words are encrypted in the same code. Can you break the code to read the names of all the tribes? As a solving aid, the words are listed in alphabetical order. For an extra hint, see the bottom of the page.

1 VTWLWXXW

2 VTSCCWPD

3 HDQJRD

4 AJY

5 TJ-VTMXQ

6 TJMBDRJXSV

7 SUJNMJSB

8 QSVQDCJJ

9 GWXJGSXWW

10 GMXBWW

11 XJNMWR

12 JESKPW

13 JXWSHD

14 JRRDPD

15 CJRDPDRJGS

16 BDMQ

17 BRJVQKUSHOWB

18 RSJXJXRDRS

19 PSXXWKDOJ

20 PLDXHJR

Hint: Number thirteen shares its name with a popular brand of flatware.

Solution on page 144.

Wisconsin "Firsts"

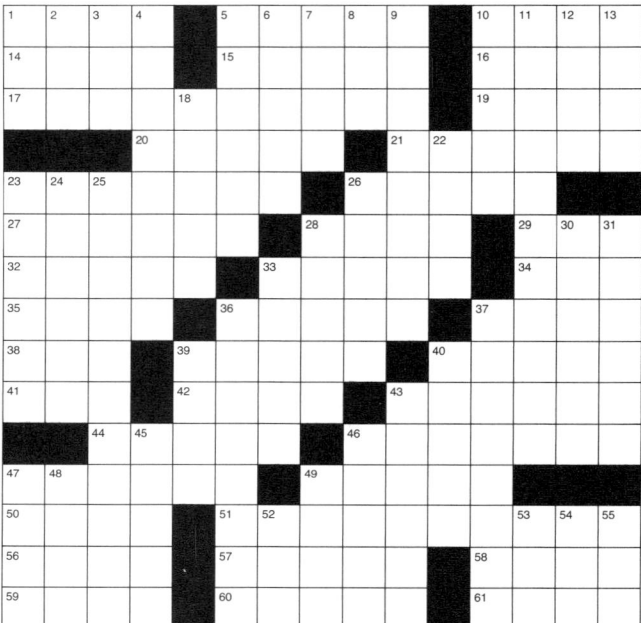

Across

1 Wisconsinite naturalist Leopold
5 Spot
10 Blue color
14 Type of ring
15 ___ a clef
16 You could get kicked to it
17 In 1873, J. W. Carhart of Racine produced the nation's first ___
19 Capital of Latvia
20 French impressionist
21 Made fair
23 Fights for
26 Card game similar to bridge
27 Expresses feelings
28 Poetic name for Ireland
29 Actress Thurman
32 ___ dinner course
33 All the world's a ___
34 ___ pons
35 Row
36 Writer Sylvia
37 Plunk
38 Secs., mins., ___
39 Direction right of sunrise
40 American industrialist John
41 Between ready and go
42 Certain Native Americans
43 The second of two

44 Not dogs' best friends
46 Shampoo brand name
47 Most arid
49 Change
50 Merit
51 Wisconsin's flag was the first state flag to travel here (2 wds.)
56 Ripened
57 Ms. Lauder
58 Name of makeup or river
59 ___ is more
60 What an usher does
61 Neck part

Down

1 Doctors' organization
2 Grant or Gehrig
3 Synonym of 5 Across
4 It can be rolled back
5 Palm parts
6 Ear parts
7 Give off
8 Baseballer Ripken
9 How tall Wisconsin corn is by the Fourth of July?
10 Farmer's units
11 The nation's first ___ were born in Watertown February 13, 1875
12 Impulse

13 He set ___ example (2 wds.)
18 Horses and lions have them
22 Tarzan's mode of transportation
23 Fatalities
24 ___ State (NY)
25 Wisconsinite Jack Vilas was the first aviator in the world to use aircraft in locating ___ (2 wds.)
26 Fury
28 Les ___ Unis
30 Demi and Michael
31 Unit of electrical current
33 Turns sharply
36 Small ___ (insignificant)
37 Wendy's friend (2 wds.)
39 Takes to court
40 Great ___ (dogs)
43 British liquid units
45 Borrows' opposite
46 Blain's Farm and ___
47 Let's Make a ___
48 Indignation
49 "___ boy!"
52 Employ
53 Actress Gardner
54 Officer of the law
55 La Crosse to Appleton direction (abbr.)

Solution on page 144.

Put the answer to the questions into the blanks provided. Then take each letter in the squares and copy them into the blanks below to answer the final question.

Wisconsin's fourth most populous city   __ __ __ __ ☐ __ __

Field where the Packers play   __ __ ☐ __ __ __ __

Popular wintertime sport invented in Wisconsin   __ __ __ __ __ ☐ __ __ __ __ __ __

Wisconsin's tallest building,

the US Bank Building, is in this city   __ __ __ __ __ __ ☐ __ __

Famous pianist from Wisconsin   __ __ __ __ __ __ __ ☐

'70s TV show set in Wisconsin   __ __ __ __ ☐ __ __ __ __

Wisconsin's largest lake   __ __ __ __ __ ☐ __ __ __

Political movement popular in Wisconsin
in the early 1900s   __ __ __ __ __ ☐ __ __ __ __ __

Wisconsin's state dog is the
American Water _____   __ __ ☐ __ __ __ __

Recreational spots that Wisconsin Dells
is famous for   __ __ __ __ ☐ __ __ __ __ __

Milwaukee's General ___ International Airport   __ __ __ ☐ __ __ __ __

Madison sits between lakes Mendota and ___   __ ☐ __ __ __ __ __

Traditional clothing company based
in Dodgeville   __ __ __ __ ☐ __ __ __

Wisconsin private college named after
an early explorer   __ __ __ __ __ __ ☐ __ __

Brewer announcer Bob ___   ☐ __ __ __ __ __

Wisconsin city, river, and county named for

this Native American tribe   __ __ __ __ ☐ __ __ __ __

Wisconsinite's term for a drinking fountain   __ __ __ __ __ ☐ __

Wisconsin's DNR developed the first

__ __ __ __ __ __   __ __ __ __   __ __ __ __ __ __ __

Across

1 Fervor
5 Bores
9 Dick and Jane's dog
13 An Exxon Mobil brand name
14 Refrain in a children's song
16 Sheltered bay
17 "Do ___ others..."
18 Literary style
19 Kids' moms
20 Wisconsin was the first state to pass a ___ law (2 wds.)
22 Greasy spoons
24 Young boy
25 Word before box or joint
26 Civil War weapon
30 Superman garment
31 Remit
34 Having an IOU
35 Plasma
36 DiCaprio nickname
37 Lion's hair
38 Actor Karloff
39 Listen!
40 *Come as You* ___
41 Employs
42 Character in *Aladdin*
43 Unit of play in tennis
44 Imitates
45 Word on an old West poster
46 .80 ___ equals one dollar

48 Ballet step
49 Fuel type
51 Wisconsin was the first state to number its ___
56 Mediterranean volcano
57 Keep your head ___ water
59 ___ *a Kick out of You* (2 wds.)
60 Wine province in Italy
61 King
62 Baseball manager Rose
63 *Wizard of Oz* actor Bert
64 Lairs
65 Fix the copy

Down

1 Olympian god
2 Serf
3 Nick and Nora's dog
4 Booty
5 Sea near Turkey
6 Exert, as in power
7 Ash Wednesday to Holy Saturday
8 Mister
9 Something to cause or steal
10 The nation's first ___ was at Fox River Rapids in Appleton (2 wds.)
11 Done
12 ___ *of the d'Urbervilles*

15 Mythical king of Thebes
21 Online journal
23 Entry on a list
25 Former Mrs. Niles Crane
26 Catalepsies
27 Knowledgeable
28 Wisconsin was the first state to ratify the ___ Amendment, giving women the right to vote
29 180 degrees from SSW
30 Goddess of agriculture
32 Hawk's nest
33 Teamed, like oxen
35 Afflictions
38 Personality disorder
39 Rooster's mate
41 Who the tortoise beats
42 Cut
45 Bets
47 Airline headquartered in Tempe (2 wds.)
48 Actor Jeremy of *Entourage*
49 Bargain
50 ___ *Small World* (2 wds.)
51 Pit
52 Use a rag
53 Got older
54 Abominable snowman
55 Leave it be
58 Miller competitor

Solution on page 144.

Across

1 United ___ Emirates
5 Dishonest men
9 The statue of Forward on the capitol dome holds a ___ in her hand
14 Central area of a church
15 4840 square yards
16 Patronage
17 Dr. Pavlov
18 Melt
19 Aired again
20 Big ___ Conference
21 Traffic ___
23 Direction of Eau Claire from the Twin Cities
24 Collector's item
27 Edge
29 What is housed in the capitol's east wing (2 wds.)
35 Major division in a long poem
38 Long time
39 Double-reed instrument
40 Woodcutter ___ Baba
41 Ital. physicist Count Alessandro ___
43 NASA's partner in SOHO
44 Ship
46 Rather than
47 Relating to the ear
49 What is housed in the capitol's north wing (2 wds.)

53 *Every Breath ___ Take*
54 Aged
58 Basketball official
61 It's not a river in Egypt
64 Lemon ender
65 Politician Stevenson
67 Pony up
68 Increase
69 The K in AKA
70 Bakery job
71 At any time
72 What is perched on 9 Across
73 Boys
74 Erase

Down

1 Singer Baker
2 Poe's bird
3 ___ garde
4 London's Big ___
5 Condiment
6 More sore
7 Lug
8 Stitched
9 It wards off vampires
10 Filmmaker Spike
11 Giant in folklore
12 Prejudice
13 Laborer
22 Sports stadium
25 Ideal or real ending

26 Status ___
28 What Elsie says
30 Certain fisherman
31 Bon ___ (witty remark)
32 German for "above"
33 Ms. Parks
34 Bluish hue
35 The Man in Black
36 Toward the sheltered side
37 Ship of 1492
41 Change of ___
42 Assoc.
45 Arid
47 Unit of electric current
48 Take or consume
50 Wound antiseptic
51 Spoke
52 Former Houston team
55 Unsophisticated
56 Henry Ford's son
57 Cast-steel plow creator John
58 Garden implement
59 Appleton author Ferber
60 Cane
62 It takes polish
63 South American empire of the 1400s
66 Woodworking tool
68 Wine selection

Robin Level

1 What is the space below the dome inside the capitol called?

2 In what decade did the capitol undergo extensive renovations?

3 What event occurs on the capitol lawn Wednesday evenings in the summer?

Musky Level

4 What major event occurred at the capitol in 1904?

5 In which city was Wisconsin's first capitol?

6 Wisconsin's capitol is the only dome in the US made of what material?

Badger Level

7 What sits on the helmet of the Forward statue perched atop the state capitol?

8 On what floor of the capitol is the observation deck?

9 Which governor was the first to hold office in the modern capitol building?

Solution on page 144.

Across

1 Pilot
6 Scratch
10 Tackle
14 Major artery
15 Hawaiian dance
16 Singing voice
17 Actress Sarandon
18 Wallach and Whitney
19 Tilt
20 Sault ___ Marie (abbr.)
21 Clock face
23 Trouble
25 Group of seniors (abbr.)
26 They sang *Dancing Queen*
27 Suspend
30 Actress Elisabeth
31 Hallucinogen
34 Projecting window
35 Swiss ___ (vegetable)
36 Single
37 Tibetan oxen
38 Barb
39 Increased
40 Little white ___
41 In the lead
42 Recipient
43 Chicago trains
44 Price
45 Cranky
46 Weapons
47 Christmas or apple
48 Napping

51 Predator opposite
52 Used to be
55 22nd letters
56 Remain
58 Banquet
60 Hodgepodge
61 Mistake exclamation
62 Disentangle
63 Paper ___
64 Tidy
65 "What is the thermostat ___?" (2 wds.)

Down

1 Back talk
2 Advertise
3 Celtic
4 Airport abbr.
5 WI governor with Civil War training camp named for him
6 Inexpensive
7 Ebb
8 Noted boxer
9 WI governor with UW-Madison's observatory named for him
10 Light wood
11 Lagers
12 Font style (abbr.)
13 Pitch
22 Wrath
24 Sleeping

25 Eras
26 Between a rock and ___ place (2 wds.)
27 Current WI governor
28 Rode out of town on ___ (2 wds.)
29 Sneakers (var.)
30 Young pig
31 SNL producer Michaels
32 Deride
33 First WI governor
35 Game of strategy
38 WI governor who left to become Secretary of HHS
39 Absent
41 Farm measurement
42 WI governor and former Chancellor of UW-Stevens Point
45 Mine output
46 He wrote fables
47 Rendezvous
48 Declare
49 Actress Ward
50 Hawaiian neckwear (pl.)
51 Father
52 Steam engine developer James
53 Largest continent
54 Let it stand
57 Digit
59 Compass abbr.

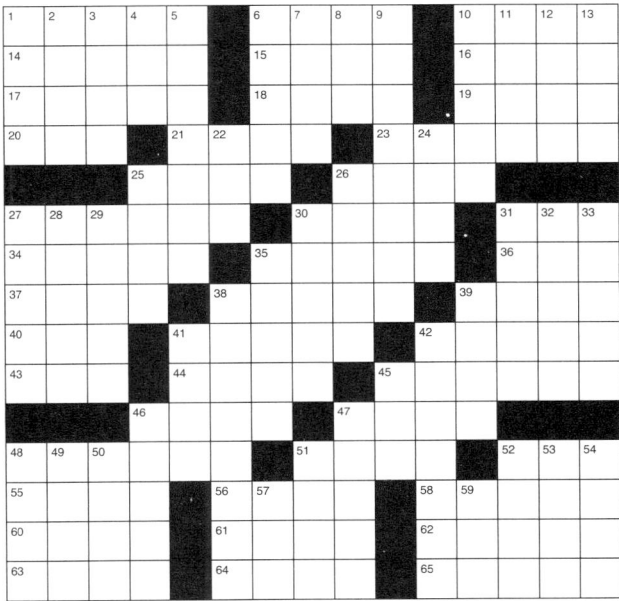

Solution on page 145.

Robin Level

1 Who was the most famous Wisconsin senator who targeted "communist sympathizers"?

2 Which political party was founded in Ripon, Wisconsin, in 1854?

3 Wisconsin was the first state to require that this be installed in all cars sold beginning in 1962.

Musky Level

4 How many members of the US House of Representatives is Wisconsin allotted?

5 What was the name of the political movement and party that gained much popularity in Wisconsin in the early 1900s?

6 Why did governor-elect Orland Steen Loomis never get to serve as governor?

Badger Level

7 How many members are in the Wisconsin State Assembly?

8 How did Governor Louis Harvey die while visiting Wisconsin troops in the Civil War?

9 Which governor's mother was one of the first women to serve in the Wisconsin legislature?

 Solution on page 144.

Seven Wisconsin politicians, past and present, are listed below in alphabetical order. Read the quotes that follow and try to match them to the politician who said them.

Gaylord Nelson   **Russ Feingold**
Herb Kohl   **Scott McCallum**
Jim Doyle   **Tommy Thompson**
Robert M. La Follette

1 From cutting back on state contracts to reducing the number of state cars, we're making state government smaller, smarter, more efficient, and more accountable.

2 If there is no sufficient reason for war, the war party will make war on one pretext, then invent another . . . after the war is on.

3 We need to fight the plague of the uninsured the way we have fought other threats to our way of life and our basic values.

4 Politicians are no different than the rest of the public.

5 Unfair trade agreements, passed by both Republicans and Democrats, have sent millions of jobs to other countries. We need to stop this hemorrhaging and find ways for American workers to compete in the new world market.

6 Wisconsin stands to become America's Biotech Prairie and we mustn't let one high tech company escape our state in search of a better climate.

7 The most important environmental issue is one that is rarely mentioned, and that is the lack of a conservation ethic in our culture.

Solution on page 145.

More political quotes are encrypted below. Find the letter substitution code for each cryptoquote to reveal the quote and the person who spoke the quote. Each code's solution is unique.

1 JK M'OB TIZBC KJMN, LMKGTCKMC'K QYBJZBKZ
KZYBCQZW GTCZMCDBK ZT SB ZWB NBNMGJZBN,
WJYNLTYPMCQ XBTXFB TI TDY KZJZB. ZWBH QT ZT
LTYP BOBYHNJH, XJH ZWBMY ZJRBK, JCN YJMKB
ZWBMY PMNK LMZW QTTN, UMNLBKZBYC OJFDBK.

— AMU NTHFB

2 IOPNP'W M ZKI KD WINPWW GXBKZBPH QOPX
LKYN OKYWP GW YXHPNQMIPN.

— WUKII AUUMZZYA, GX M DZKKHPH
TNMGNGP HY UOGPX

3 YVJ FQYLDHYJ YJIY KW DHZ'I EKZIELJZEJ DHP
RJ VLI CLQQLZBZJII YK IHEXLWLEJ IKDJYVLZB
YKOHP WKX WFYFXJ BJZJXHYLKZI CVKIJ CKXOI
KW YVHZUI CLQQ ZKY RJ VJHXO.

— BHPQKXO ZJQIKZ

4 TUH BLG ZXTG UT EG, X MPSSUB YSWGHVBPSW
CLQ BLG BGHHUHXVBV LPIG SUB PBBPMRGW
UYH TUUW VYAAZQ FGMPYVG XB XV VU GPVQ
BU WU.

— BUEEQ BLUEAVUS

5 QSKFZYQWA RQWO OB VKMKQO OKFFBFZAS
QWV ODKL RQWO ODK JQAZY YDQFQYOKF BM
ODZA YBXWOFL OB AXFEZEK QWV HFBAHKF.
ODKL RQWO JBOD AKYXFZOL QWV UZJKFOL,
QWV XWUKAA RK PZEK ODKS JBOD — QWV RK
YQW ZM RK OFL — RK DQEK MQZUKV.

— FXAA MKZWPBUV

Solution on page 145.

Across

1 Mary-Kate or Ashley
6 Church part
10 Seize
14 Languages of southern Africa
15 Joint between fabrics
16 *Penny* ___
17 Newton or Asimov
18 In Brookfield, ___ is illegal unless done for medical purposes
20 Sixth sense
21 Plant in the onion family
23 Hay bundles
24 Sweetie
25 Ezra Pound, for one
27 Rerun
30 Styles
31 Picnic crasher
34 Former Houston player
35 What Marquette traveled in
36 ___-Jones average
37 Eden inhabitant
38 Serious
39 Fix
40 Allow
41 "___ we dance?"
42 Quiz answer
43 Rapper Dr. ___
44 Model
45 Realty ad: "Just ___!"
46 ___ Rite

47 Employ
48 Stair part
51 Type of organ
52 Baseball bat wood
55 In La Crosse, it is illegal to display an ___ mannequin in a store window
58 Flick
60 Doc's ASAP
61 Had on
62 Singer Baker
63 Pop
64 Chooses
65 "We shall ___ forget"

Down

1 Off-Broadway award
2 Girl
3 Cinch
4 JFK info
5 In Sun Prairie, ___ weapons may not be manufactured in the city limits
6 Fall bloomer
7 Mountain top
8 Took a seat
9 Ambulance worker (abbr.)
10 Dwell with satisfaction
11 Before road or way
12 Ms. Frank
13 Pleads

19 Body weight 20% greater than recommended
22 "___ your heart out"
24 Judge
25 Committee
26 Smell
27 Author Dahl
28 Type of down
29 Home ___
30 Short moral story
31 Mature
32 Relating to Scandinavia
33 Type of jacket
35 Move effortlessly
38 Before box or lace
39 What a detective works on
41 VP Agnew
42 In Racine, it is illegal to wake a ___ when he is asleep
45 Sass
46 Area near a river's mouth
47 Animal skins
48 Senator Feingold
49 ___ *Thin Air*
50 Multitude
51 Irreverent
52 Tel ___
53 Location
54 Listen
56 ___ Rivers, Wisconsin
57 Type of scotch?
59 The loneliest number

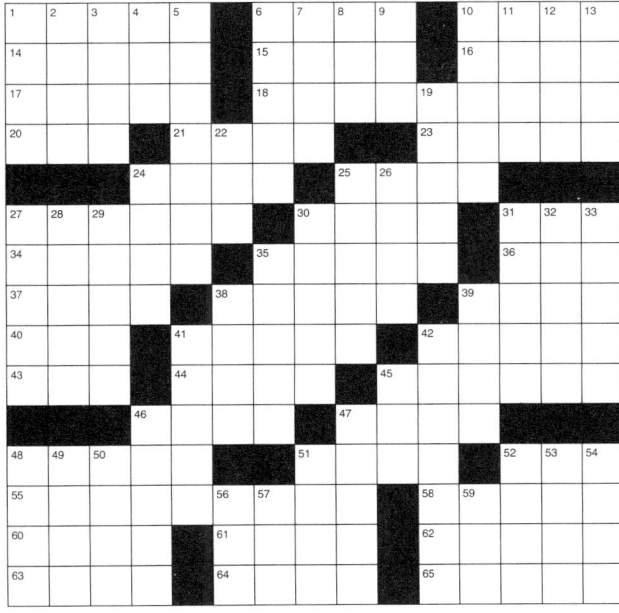

Solution on page 145.

More Strange Laws

Complete the sentence by filling in the blank with the words on the right to discover a current or former law.

1 In Wisconsin, it is illegal to serve an apple pie in public restaurants without ___.

2 In Hudson, ___ are required on all windows from May 1 to October 1.

3 In Wisconsin, it is illegal to ___ at a railroad car.

4 In Racine, ___ may not be shot at parade participants.

5 In St. Croix, women are not allowed to wear anything ___ in public.

6 In Sun Prairie, cats are forbidden in ___.

7 In Wisconsin, you must manually ___ all urinals in a building.

8 In La Crosse, it is illegal to ___ in public.

9 In Wisconsin, it is illegal to serve ___ in state prisons.

10 In Milwaukee, if someone is thought of as offensive looking, it is illegal for him or her to ___ during the day.

11 In La Crosse, it is illegal to "worry a ___."

12 In Wisconsin, it is illegal to ___ on a train.

13 In Milwaukee, it is against the law to ___ on the streets to attract attention.

14 In La Crosse, it is illegal to ___ along Third Street.

15 In Wisconsin, ___ have the right-of-way on public roads.

A flush

B tie up your horse

C cut a woman's hair

D screens

E livestock

F missiles

G play checkers

H squirrel

I red

J play a flute and drums

K throw rocks

L butter substitutes

M cemeteries

N be in public

O cheese

Solution on page 145.

R	E	S			
O	L		T	A	L
L	F	I	**FOOD**		D
W	I	**FAME**		O	N
O	N	T	O	B	U
A	I	L	**&**	E	G
K	**FUN**		S	T	O
	S	R	P	E	N
N		L	A	D	E
F	A		R	T	R

Wisconsin is famous for its food. Anyone's palate will find something pleasing in the assortment of homegrown delights—world-famous breweries, bumper crops of cherries and cranberries, and squeaky-fresh cheese curds, to name a few.

Speaking of famous, many Wisconsinites have gone out into the world and made their home state proud. Television and film actors and actresses got their starts here, and a love of Wisconsin has led many shows and movies to use the state as their backdrop or setting. Some Wisconsinites have gone much farther than Hollywood, however. There are those who have made it beyond Earth itself. At least eight astronauts once called Wisconsin home.

And then there are those who never left Wisconsin at all. Even in death some Wisconsinites just aren't ready to exit our great state. In almost every town, local historians can recall a ghost story or two, and numerous books have been penned on the subject. Spooky folklore is so embedded in our society that Kaukauna High School's mascot is a Galloping Ghost.

Across

1 He does stand-up
6 Or ___!
10 Male cow
14 Ancient Greek marketplace
15 Serf
16 India's continent
17 Doze
18 ___ Brewing, Black River Falls
20 "...nine, ten, a big fat ___"
21 Golf club
23 Swarm
24 Type of bomb
25 Bridge
27 ___ Microbrewery, Tomahawk
30 Superman or Batman, e.g.
31 Type of tub
34 Relating to the ear
35 He had the golden touch
36 ___ Hill (elite area)
37 Rigel or Betelgeuse, e.g.
38 Sir's counterpart
39 Bucket
40 Packers' scores (abbr.)
41 Warning device
42 Din
43 Cry for help (abbr.)
44 Towel word
45 ___ Brewing, Milwaukee
46 A host of
47 Before "and call"

48 Diner
51 Fodder storage
52 Also
55 ___ Brewing, Superior (2 wds.)
58 What a student should do
60 God of war
61 Cliff Huxtable's son
62 Person with the mic
63 Vega's constellation
64 Village
65 Instructor

Down

1 Singer Johnny
2 Eye
3 Kohler competitor
4 Anger
5 ___ Brewery, Middleton
6 Type of salt
7 Without much fat
8 Michael, to Kirk
9 Finale
10 Nobleman
11 Manipulator
12 Deceived
13 Superior or Michigan, e.g.
19 Ado
22 CD-___
24 Open
25 Car

26 Baby buggy
27 Survives
28 Surmount
29 The ___ is always greener
30 Conceals
31 Mollusk with a spiral shell
32 What a beauty queen has
33 More fit
35 Wed
38 Aspect
39 11th president
41 Knife adjective
42 ___ Brewing, Florence
45 Actor Gibson
46 Genius group
47 Great Plains animal
48 And others (abbr. 2 wds.)
49 Off course
50 Layer
51 Hearty soup
52 Diplomacy
53 "Milk's Favorite Cookie"
54 Doozy
56 Baseball's "Boy Wonder"
57 17th letter of Greek alphabet
59 Flightless bird

Solution on page 145.

Robin Level

1 Which immigrants brought their beer-making knowledge to Wisconsin?

2 In the state of Wisconsin, what is the minimum blood alcohol content at which one is considered to be operating while intoxicated?

3 What kind of beer is fermented with bottom-fermenting yeasts at lower temperatures for longer times, sometimes resulting in darker hues?

Musky Level

4 At one time, the world's four largest breweries were all located in Milwaukee. Name three of them.

5 Which Wisconsin beer manufacturer has the registered trademark "The Flavor of the Northwoods"?

6 In what city will you find the world's largest six-pack?

Badger Level

7 What was the name of the mythical creature that William T. Cox invented to keep his lumberjacks from sneaking off to drink at night?

8 What is the only university in Wisconsin with a brewhouse for public consumption?

9 What Wisconsin county was originally created as a "dry" county in 1839 and named after a prominent eastern temperance leader?

Solution on page 144.

Fill all empty squares so that the nine letters appear once in each row, column, and 3x3 box. The answer, reading across the middle row, will reveal the name of a keg used in home brewing.

		S	U					I
	E				R	C		
	C				N			L
	S	E		R	U	L	N	
	L	U	S	C		R	O	
O			E				I	
		L	U				C	
S				I		E		

Across

1 Berets
5 Seat
10 Word on a gift tag
14 Unwritten
15 Inflict a heavy blow
16 Puerto ___
17 Fresh
18 Oktoberfest's illuminated ___ Parade
20 One who dallies
22 NY ballpark
23 Annoy
24 Principle
27 Hurray
28 ___ Moines, IA
29 Pale lager
32 Vat
34 Wisconsin Dells to Fond du Lac direction
35 *Green* ___
37 Toy sticks
41 Remote
43 Sun (prefix)
45 *A Star Is* ___
46 Couches
48 18th Greek letter
50 Actress Thompson
51 Apiece
53 Fair fare (2 wds.)
55 Revolutionary Adams

58 Certain beer color
60 Platform
61 "Are you a man ___ mouse?" (2 wds.)
62 Flying saucers
64 Type of tube
67 Oktoberfest's official celebrant
71 Sooner State (abbr.)
72 Author unknown (abbr.)
73 End
74 ___ Martin cognac
75 Harangue
76 ___ Park, Colorado
77 Feelings of self-importance

Down

1 Actress Spelling
2 Dry
3 Oktoberfest's Saturday afternoon ___ Parade (2 wds.)
4 Rains with ice
5 WI's time zone
6 Group ins.
7 Put on ___
8 Restless
9 Use a microwave
10 Before Sat.
11 Stiff
12 Yellow-orange
13 Specks

19 Basketball shot
21 Mother of Zeus
25 Small measurement
26 Largest asteroid
29 Like two ___ in a pod
30 Data
31 Memento
33 The "Fighting" La Follette
36 Breathes out heavily
38 Oktoberfest opens with the tapping of the ___ (2 wds.)
39 Cookie eaten with milk
40 Catch
42 Ice T's music
44 Leave out
47 Potion
49 Jai ___
52 Change the cabinet doors
54 Pretend not to hear
55 ___, so good (2 wds.)
56 Milwaukee's US Cellular ___
57 Bricklayer
59 Quantities of medicine
63 ASAP to a Dr.
65 *Sesame Street* favorite
66 Beams
68 Blast initials
69 Superior to Minocqua direction
70 Hi-___ photo

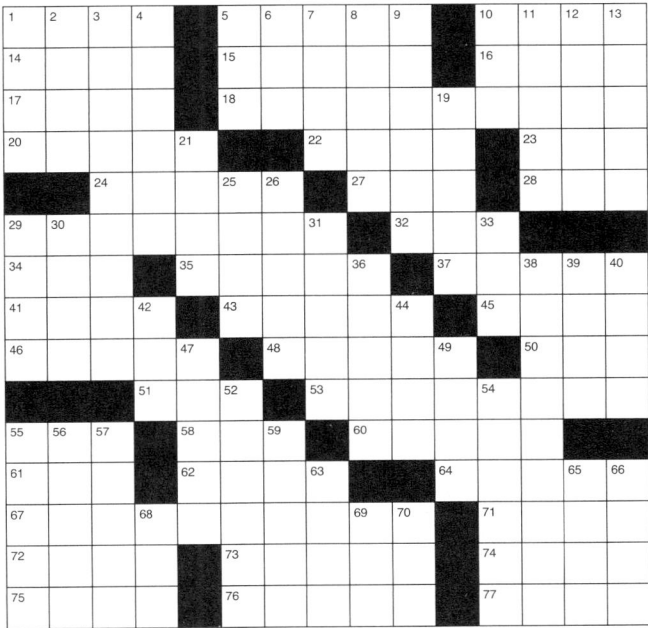

Solution on page 146.

All the words below are names of food that come from Wisconsin. The words are encrypted in the same code. Can you break the code to read the names of all the foods? As a solving aid, the words are listed in alphabetical order. For an extra hint, see the bottom of the page.

1 HZZR

2 HVLXAJVBX

3 HJXXZV

4 UTZZBZ

5 UTZVVQZB

6 UDVK

7 UVLKHZVVQZB

8 ZFFB

9 FQKBZKF

10 TDKZN

11 QUZ UVZLS

12 SLWIZ BNVJW

13 SQIE

14 WDXLXDZB

15 BLJBLFZ

16 BDN HZLKB

17 XVDJX

18 XJVEZN

19 ALIIZNZ

20 AQIG VQUZ

Hint: As a popular Wendy's commercial used to ask, "Where's the ___?" Try number one.

Solution on page 146.

Robin Level

1 Which one of these cannot be found in Wisconsin: a honey museum, a mustard museum, or a ketchup museum?

2 The Chalet Cheese Co-Op in Monroe is the only place in the US that still makes this kind of cheese.

3 What is the name for the outdoor cooking events in Door County?

Musky Level

4 What type of dessert was created in Two Rivers in 1881?

5 Name one of the two treats first created by Racine's Horlick Malt Company.

6 What national fast food chain started in Sauk City, Wisconsin?

Badger Level

7 What kind of margarine was illegal to sell in Wisconsin until 1967?

8 Wisconsin consumes 90 percent of what beverage produced in the US?

9 The Waterloo company Van Holten Inc. is the nation's only distributor of what food in a pouch?

Solution on page 146.

From Wisconsin to Hollywood

Across

1 Jane Austen novel
5 Pasture noises
9 Comes closer
14 Meadows
15 A shake's cousin
16 Believe it ___ (2 wds.)
17 Carroll College football player and *My Three Sons* actor Fred ___
19 Wed
20 Fat substitute found in chips
21 Beat
23 Hog
24 Philbin's cohost
27 Pencil ends
29 Madison native and *The West Wing* actor Bradley ___, married to 69 Across
33 JFK abbr.
34 Transmit
35 Affirmatives
37 ___ the Sheriff
41 Kind of milk
43 Back tooth
45 Bread of Holy Communion
46 100 centavos
47 Second generation Japanese American
49 Pasture noise
50 Place for story time
53 Green Bay native and *Monk* actor Tony ___

55 King Arthur's kingdom
59 Solo
60 ___ carte (2 wds.)
61 Apple's portable audio player
63 Mountains dividing Russia
67 Author ___ Luis Borge
69 Milwaukee native and *Malcolm in the Middle* actress Jane ___, married to 29 Across
72 Worker's guild
73 Charles Lamb's pen name
74 Pop
75 Demands
76 Type of tide
77 Catch

Down

1 Furry red monster
2 ___ ticket
3 Defensive spray
4 "She's ___ cookie" (2 wds.)
5 Childhood vaccine (abbr.)
6 Paddle
7 The Count in *A Series of Unfortunate Events*
8 Flair
9 Candy bar center
10 Sea bird
11 Flavorful seed
12 Helicopter part

13 Frets
18 Become one
22 100 ___ equal 1 krona
25 What 67 Across wrote
26 Intentional blaze
28 Belt
29 Hornet kin
30 Increase in cost
31 Bulb bloomer
32 Sandwich shops
36 Ice skater Cohen
38 Vagrant
39 Jacob's twin
40 ___ in the back
42 Spy
44 Back
48 Site of the Trojan War
51 Little green men
52 Small explosion
54 Bother
55 Southern cuisine
56 Solo
57 Queen ___ Antoinette
58 Arcade coin
62 Open river valley
64 Elvis's middle name
65 Helen of Troy's mother
66 Heroin
68 Deity
70 Porter Goss is its current director
71 Lightning strike

116   Solution on page 146.

The Acting Bug Bites Wisconsin

Match the Wisconsin-connected actors and actresses with their mini bios.

1 Arnold Schwarzenegger

2 Charlotte Rae

3 Chris Farley

4 Gary Burghoff

5 Gena Rowlands

6 Gene Wilder

7 Harrison Ford

8 Heather Graham

9 Jackie Mason

10 Judith Light

11 Kristen Johnston

12 Spencer Tracy

13 Tom Wopat

14 Tyne Daly

A Lived in Milwaukee while working in a repertory company there, played Angela Bower on *Who's the Boss?*

B Born in Madison, played Mary Beth Lacey in *Cagney and Lacey* and Maxine Gray on *Judging Amy*.

C Grew up in Lodi and played Luke Duke on *The Dukes of Hazzard*.

D Went to high school in Delavan and played Radar O'Reilly on *M*A*S*H*.

E Grew up in Milwaukee and played Willy Wonka in *Willy Wonka and the Chocolate Factory*.

F Milwaukee native who won two Oscars, was a longtime companion of Katharine Hepburn, and made nine films with her.

G Born in Milwaukee and played Mrs. Garrett on *The Facts of Life*.

H Stand-up comedian and rabbi who was born in Sheboygan and starred in *Caddyshack II*.

I Madison native who became famous on *Saturday Night Live* and starred in *Tommy Boy*.

J Daughter of a Wisconsin state legislator who starred in *The Notebook*.

K Graduated from Whitefish Bay High School and played Sally Solomon in *3rd Rock from the Sun*.

L Born in Milwaukee and played Felicity Shagwell in *Austin Powers: The Spy Who Shagged Me*.

M Attended Ripon College and made such blockbusters as *Star Wars*, *Raiders of the Lost Ark*, and *The Fugitive*.

N UW-Superior graduate and star of *The Terminator*.

Hollywood Quote Game

To read the following four quotes from the Wisconsin-connected actors, you must first solve the clues below. Put the answer on the blanks and then transfer the letters into the grid above according to the number under its blank. Work back and forth to solve.

1C		2B	3F	4D	5E		6A	7B	8E	9B	10D	11F		12F	13D	14C	15G	16A
17C	18E		19D	20B	21C	22D		23B	24C		25A	26E	27G		28A	29E	30F	31B
32E	33G		34E	35A		36C	37D	38G	39B		40G	41E	42B	43F	44A	45E		46F
	47B	48E	49D		50G	51C	52A	53D	54F	55C	56B	57D	58E					

— Quote by Jackie Mason

A _ _ _ _ _ _ _
52 16 44 25 6 28 35 — Agatha Christie's genre

B _ _ _ _ _ _ _ _ _ _
31 2 9 23 47 39 42 56 7 20 — Hans Christian Andersen tale

C _ _ _ _ _ _ _ _
55 51 36 21 17 24 1 14 — Black-and-white dairy cow

D _ _ _ _ _ _ _ _ _
19 13 57 10 53 4 37 22 49 — Lifespan

E _ _ _ _ _ _ _ _ _ _ _
26 8 34 18 58 5 41 29 32 48 45 — The same throughout

F _ _ _ _ _ _ _
3 54 11 43 46 30 12 — Disbelief in God

G _ _ _ _ _ _
15 33 38 40 50 27 — Flow out

1F	2E	3G	4B	5D	6A	7C	8G	9C		10F		11F	12G	13A	14D		15C	16F	17H
18G		19E	20B	21F		22C	23D	24G	25E	26F	27D	28A	29B	30D		31C		32B	33H
34C	35D		36G	37B	38C	39E		40C	41A	42G		43D	44E		45H	46G	47D	48F	49H
50E	51B	52A	53F		54B	55G	56D	57B	58H	59D	60F								

— Quote by Chris Farley

A _ _ _ _ _
13 6 28 41 52 — A dead language

B _ _ _ _ _ _ _ _
32 57 54 29 20 4 37 51 — Word before diabetes or delinquency

C _ _ _ _ _ _ _ _
15 40 9 34 31 22 38 7 — *Let's Get* ___ by Olivia Newton John

D _ _ _ _ _ _ _ _ _ _
47 56 14 5 43 35 27 23 59 30 — A bird that eats insects on the wing

E _ _ _ _ _ _
50 19 44 2 25 39 — Old type of phone

F _ _ _ _ _ _ _ _ _
16 10 48 21 1 11 26 53 60 — What the *Titanic* needed more of

G _ _ _ _ _ _ _ _ _
55 8 18 42 36 46 24 12 3 — Dan Jansen and Bonnie Blair

H _ _ _ _ _
58 17 33 45 49 — Bea Arthur character and TV show

Solution on page 148.

1B		2G	3A	4H	5C		6A	7D	8B		9E	10H	11C		12B	13G	14A	15F	16H
17E	18C	19E	20F	21B		22A	23E	24B	25C	26F	27H		28B	29E		30A	31B	32E	33G
	34G	35D	36A		37D	38F	39G	40A		41B	42F	43G	44F	45H	46B	47G		48B	49C
50A	51C	52D	53F		54B	55E		56A	57B	58D	59G	60E	61H						

— Quote by Harrison Ford

A ___ ___ ___ ___ ___ ___ ___ ___ ___
30 56 14 22 50 3 6 40 36
Dwelling by a barn

B ___ ___ ___ ___ ___ ___ ___ ___ ___ ___ ___ ___
12 31 8 48 57 21 28 41 24 1 54 46
Not over-the-counter

C ___ ___ ___ ___ ___ ___
5 51 18 49 25 11
Thin-skinned

D ___ ___ ___ ___ ___
7 37 52 58 35
Slow two-toed tree creature

E ___ ___ ___ ___ ___ ___ ___ ___
55 19 9 29 23 60 17 32
Spanish dance

F ___ ___ ___ ___ ___ ___ ___
53 26 42 38 15 44 20
Country singer Lynn

G ___ ___ ___ ___ ___ ___ ___ ___
13 2 33 59 34 39 43 47
Confessed

H ___ ___ ___ ___ ___ ___
45 4 27 16 10 61
Conclusion

1D	2J	3E	4A	5B		6B	7D	8E	9A		10H	11E	12J	13F	14D		15D	16A	17C
18G		19G	20J		21C	22I	23G	24J	25D		26F	27D	28A	29H		30H	31E		32I
33F	34D	35E		36G		37E	38H	39C	40B	41E		42A	43G	44E		45C	46E		47G
	48B	49I	50H	51A		52B	53I	54F		55F	56D	57E	58C		59E	60C		61F	62I
63H	64I	65F		66I	67A	68G	69B	70J		71H	72C		73G	74A	75I	76C	77D		

— Quote by Spencer Tracy

A ___ ___ ___ ___ ___ ___ ___ ___
4 67 16 51 74 28 42 9
Practice

B ___ ___ ___ ___ ___ ___
6 52 48 69 40 5
Move like a duck

C ___ ___ ___ ___ ___ ___ ___ ___
21 45 58 17 72 60 39 76
With strength or authority

D ___ ___ ___ ___ ___ ___ ___ ___ ___
15 34 1 56 7 14 77 27 25
Testifiers in court

E ___ ___ ___ ___ ___ ___ ___ ___ ___ ___ ___
37 57 46 41 59 44 11 31 35 3 8
Product used after shampoo

F ___ ___ ___ ___ ___ ___ ___
26 33 61 65 55 13 54
Used an egg beater

G ___ ___ ___ ___ ___ ___ ___ ___
19 68 43 23 73 47 36 18
Keep in good condition

H ___ ___ ___ ___ ___ ___ ___
10 63 38 30 71 50 29
Pair

I ___ ___ ___ ___ ___ ___ ___ ___
62 64 66 75 32 49 22 53
Inhabitant of a South Pacific island

J ___ ___ ___ ___ ___
12 20 24 2 70
Folklore

Solution on page 148.

Hollywood Bigwigs from Wisconsin

Across
1 Raised wound
5 Bit at
11 ___ Hot Ballroom
14 Mammalian covering
15 Georgian ruler Shevardnadze
16 Perfect serve
17 Movie director from Kenosha (2 wds.)
19 War of ___ Worlds
20 Complete
21 Attention-getting sound
22 First-responders gp.
25 ...Fa, ___, La...
26 Prison
29 Waukesha native and owner of motion picture production companies Harry ___
31 The Barefoot ___
35 Haddock
36 Escapes
37 2001 computer
38 Cupid counterpart
39 Iran-Contra Affair figure North
40 Diplomacy
41 Toss
42 Shovel
43 Turkish authority (var.)
44 1992 Redford/Poitier movie
46 Brothers David and Jerry ___ from Milwaukee produced movies such as Airplane!
47 Beaujolais or Zinfandel
48 Imperfection
49 Aves.
50 Number of easy pieces?
53 Stares
55 One, prefix
56 He was a clothing store manager in Oshkosh before founding Universal Pictures in Hollywood (2 wds.)
62 My Gal ___
63 First western journalist to interview bin Laden
64 Heed
65 Madison to Watertown dir.
66 Saint ___ of Avila
67 Fence opening

Down
1 The Spy ___ Loved Me
2 Play it by ___
3 Fleur-de-___
4 Horse's gait
5 Word with Isaac or fig
6 Perfect
7 Push's opposite
8 Friend
9 Prior to
10 Letters after some dr.'s names
11 School subj.
12 What a tooth may feel
13 Name
18 Edged
21 Stout
22 Artist's stands
23 A millionth of a meter
24 Kind of light
26 Actress Angelina
27 Add your chip
28 ___ a Wonderful Life
30 Boxers' accomplishments
31 Winter maladies
32 Hovels
33 Perfumed bag
34 Worship tables
36 Make a loud noise
39 ___ Season
40 Tic ___ Toe
42 Enjoy a snowy hill
43 Blender setting
45 Amazement
46 Mexican revolutionary
48 Dairy treats
50 Igniter
51 ___ instant (2 wds.)
52 Repulsive
53 High school club
54 Unhealthy city air
56 ___ Ballou
57 We ___ Marshall
58 Goal of a vacation (abbr.)
59 Degree for a corporate worker
60 "___ freedom ring..."
61 In the public ___

Solution on page 146.

Across

1 Singer Redding
5 Fights
10 Right away
14 Mend
15 Fortuneteller's card
16 Disney's ___ & Stitch
17 Chocolate cookie
18 Fall flower
19 Actor Sharif
20 2003 movie set in rural Wisconsin (2 wds.)
22 Fireplace bottom (2 wds.)
24 Golf device
25 Crucial
26 Greek capital
30 Balcony section
31 Sixth sense
34 Plant and animal life of a region
35 Octet
36 21st letter of Greek alphabet
37 Instrument with double reed
38 Enter
39 Type of custard treat
40 Tear
41 Swing band leader Shaw
42 Go
43 Small amount
44 Lady's mate
45 French film festival locale

46 A cold and ___ day
48 Container
49 Playground equipment
51 1988 movie starring Molly Ringwald (2 wds.)
56 Ages
57 ___ Ike (2 wds.)
59 Honest
60 Lemon partner
61 What actors deliver
62 An actor's part
63 For fear that
64 Ogles
65 Sports station

Down

1 Scent
2 Balance a scale
3 Angered
4 Prig
5 The United ___
6 Out-of-date
7 Creative
8 Digit
9 The ___ Story, 1999 movie involving a tractor trip
10 Hawaiian hello
11 1998 movie starring Billy Bob Thornton, with A (2 wds.)
12 Jai ___

13 Dock
21 Italian volcano
23 Proofer's mark
25 Fashion magazine
26 Cut short
27 Leg bone
28 1994 critically acclaimed documentary
29 Summer (Fr.)
30 A type of fat
32 Trim
33 Longs (for)
35 Passage
38 1994 movie starring Kevin Spacey (2 wds.)
39 Low, swampy ground
41 Inter ___ (among other things)
42 Whim
45 Hug
47 Positive feature
48 One who teases
49 Vend
50 One of the Great Lakes
51 Penalty
52 To be (Fr.)
53 God of love
54 Soggy mass
55 Witnessed
58 Untruth

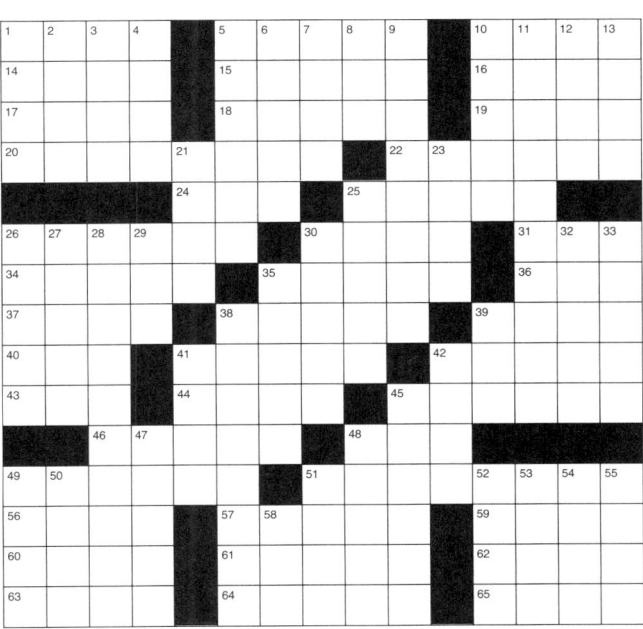

Solution on page 146.

121

Robin Level

1 This 1970s show set in suburban Milwaukee revolved around the Cunningham family.

2 A spin-off of the first show, this show set in Milwaukee was about two young female roommates with two crazy male neighbors upstairs.

3 This show, set in fictional Point Place, Wisconsin, brought stardom to all of its young cast members, including Ashton Kutcher and Topher Grace.

Musky Level

4 An hour-long drama/comedy from the mid-90s, this odd show produced by David E. Kelley was set in fictional Rome, Wisconsin, and focused on the family of the sheriff, Jimmy Brock.

5 Set in a fictional version of Genoa City, Wisconsin, this CBS daytime soap opera has been running since March of 1973.

6 Divorced parents, played by Patrick Duffy and Suzanne Somers, meet and marry and try to keep their family happy in this sitcom set in Port Washington during the 90s.

Badger Level

7 This cartoon, set in fictional Plainsville, Wisconsin, stars Rudy, a young boy whose magical piece of chalk can allow him to draw and enter a world of his creation, where he runs into everything and anything that's been drawn on a chalkboard before.

8 This unsuccessful show starring a former actor from *Cheers* was set in Madison and centered on a man with a radio show about cars.

9 Norm McDonald stars as a reporter on a TV news magazine who moves to Waterford Falls, Wisconsin, to get a chance to live the idyllic American lifestyle.

Solution on page 147.

Magazines Published in Wisconsin

Across
1 Actor Neeson
5 Country dwelling
9 Arranged
14 Sicily's Mount ___
15 Water in Spanish
16 Between (prefix)
17 Magazine about the Universe published in Waukesha
19 Suspicious
20 Short kind of poem
21 A Gallup ___
23 Actress Vardalos
24 Within (prefix)
27 Showed a response
29 ___ Collector, a magazine for particular paper lovers, published in Iola
33 Time period
34 The whole enchilada
35 Mistake
37 Dateless at a dance
41 First king of the Israelites
43 Old World tree with long seedpods
45 Artist's oven
46 Supermodel Banks
47 British actor Hawthorne
49 National campground chain
50 Neither's partner
53 Farmer's weekly journal published in Madison (hyph.)

55 Schematic drawing
59 Day after Thanksgiving event
60 Last word in stories
61 Thought
63 Develop
67 Southwestern house material
69 ___ World, for musicians with a beat, published in Madison (2 wds.)
72 Come of age
73 ___ mater
74 Organized
75 Attack (2 wds.)
76 Steady gait
77 Tool for shaping wood

Down
1 Actress Remini
2 "___ girl!" (2 wds.)
3 Against (prefix)
4 Word after stock or super
5 Enthusiast
6 A long time ___
7 Type of roast
8 Tom Barrett is Milwaukee's
9 Column
10 Ace
11 Surgical tube supporting a vessel
12 Creepy
13 Wood nymph
18 Pound division

22 ___ Harvey Oswald
25 Pours a driveway
26 Senator Hatch
28 Barrel
29 ___ tense
30 Oil of ___
31 Aspersion
32 SS Andrea ___
36 Tennis player Bobby
38 Bar or idol starter
39 Soothing plant
40 Chew on
42 The ___ Companies, décor business out of Delafield
44 Word repeated in a Doris Day song
48 Fragrant spring bush
51 Determine one's position
52 Extreme (slang)
54 City in Italy and WI
55 Sweethearts
56 Film not affiliated with a major company
57 Take as one's own
58 Decoration
62 Folk singer Guthrie
64 Troubled
65 Dweeb
66 Italian Renaissance family
68 Opie's aunt
70 Baseball official
71 Sallie or Fannie

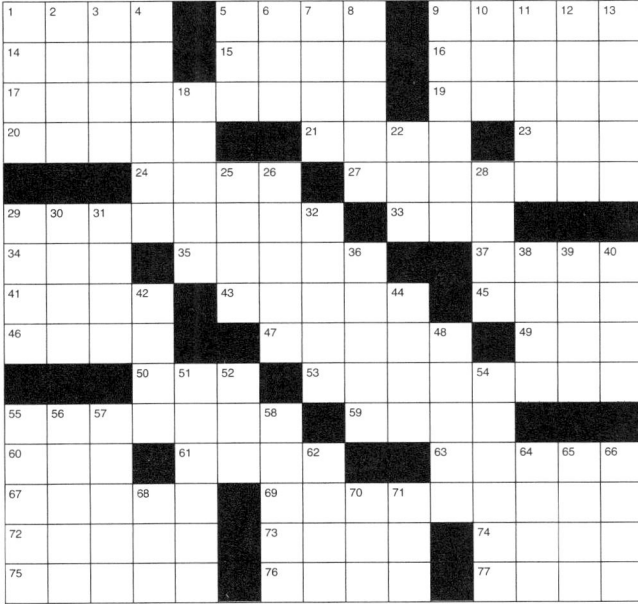

Solution on page 147.

More Publications from Wisconsin

All the words below are titles of magazines that are published in Wisconsin. The words are encrypted in the same code. Can you break the code to read the names of all the magazines? As a solving aid, the words are listed in alphabetical order. For an extra hint, see the bottom of the page.

1 DXEJDAPW

11 SYGXWGDRXK SPJW

2 DSRXTYP REDHPE

12 WXBPSR WVMERW

3 DEKRXK DSRNEMVMBMUF

13 RDWRP MC NMGP

4 QPDH WRFBP

14 RNP NDEGMSXLPE

5 QXU EPPB

15 RNP VEMUEPWWXAP

6 QXEHPE'W JMEBH

16 RNP RXGQPE VEMHYKPE

7 KNPPWP EPVMERPE

17 RNP JEXRPE

8 KMYSREF JMGDS

18 REDXSW

9 KEMV WKXPSKP

19 JXWKMSWXS MYRHMME IMYESDB

10 PDD WVMER VXBMR

20 JMEBH DXEWNMJ SPJW

Hint: Our state name can be found in number nineteen.

Solution on page 147.

Across

1 Birth related
6 Game of strategy
11 Evergreen
14 ___ Gay (WWII bomber)
15 Hawk's nest
16 Yalie
17 Snag
18 Mission specialist on STS-101 from Winter (with first initial)
20 Bit
21 Wake
23 Harvest
24 Take off of mother's milk
25 Keats' specialty
27 Rock formed from lava
30 Fever
32 TV channel offering Casablanca
35 Shenanigan
36 Bare
37 Wrath
38 Slop
39 Acme
40 ___ Park, Colorado
42 Sunbather's goal
43 Solo
45 John Philip ___, The March King
46 Unit of energy
47 Not green
48 Attacks
49 ___ out (make do)
50 Pile
51 ___ vera
54 Squalid
56 Native American from Utah area
59 Apollo 13 spacecraft commander and Milwaukee resident (2 wds.)
62 Male singing voice
64 You ___ what you eat
65 Dishwasher setting
66 Writer Nash
67 Campaigned
68 Devoured
69 Hangman's loop

Down

1 Egg's environs
2 Tennis player Kournikova
3 Frog kin
4 Extraterrestrial TV character
5 UW-Madison graduate and Racine native who perished during space shuttle reentry on 2/1/03 (2 wds.)
6 Louisiana's version of Acadian
7 Cuts
8 Great Lakes port
9 ___ vous plait
10 Salt (Fr.)
11 The ___ of Living Dangerously
12 Big Bird's friend
13 Curlicue (of smoke)
19 ___ cream
22 A grass seed
24 Lament
25 Days of ___ Lives
26 Sparta native and Apollo docking module pilot in first American-Russian space meeting (2 wds.)
27 Treat a turkey while cooking
28 Former Egyptian president Sadat
29 He sang Fields of Gold
30 Repent
31 Stare
32 1st century Emperor of Rome
33 Toothpaste brand
34 Plateaus
36 Something to do in the name of love?
41 Type of opera, like 25 Down
44 What you do in 48 Down after you make it
48 Cot
49 Slithery swimmer
50 ___ of Troy
51 Slightly open
52 Money in Malta
53 Sign
54 Mailed
55 Or ___! (threat)
56 Cancel
57 What a sandal reveals
58 European sea eagle
60 Mine quarry
61 By way of
63 Self

Solution on page 147.

125

Robin Level

1 In this movie about the search for intelligent alien life, the main character played by Jodie Foster is based on real-life SETI scientist Jill Tarter from De Pere, Wisconsin.

2 Mark Lee of Viroqua, Wisconsin, and Jan Davis of Alabama were the first what in space?

3 The flawed Hubble Space Telescope mirror was fixed through an innovative design created by researchers at what university?

Musky Level

4 Three Wisconsin cities claim to be the UFO Capital of the World. Name one.

5 In the movie *Apollo 13*, Jim Lovell's son watches the events unfold on television from a classroom at which school in Delafield, Wisconsin?

6 Yerkes Observatory in Williams Bay is home to the world's largest what?

Badger Level

7 The Astronautics Corporation of America, which creates the High Accuracy Inertial Navigation System for the Space Shuttle, is headquartered in which Wisconsin city?

8 Senator Joe Leibham of Sheboygan proposes creating what kind of facility on the shore of Lake Michigan?

9 On September 6, 1962, a piece of what crashed onto a downtown street in Manitowoc?

Solution on page 147.

Across

1 ___ Lake, Oneida County
6 ___, Marathon County
10 Destruction
14 It's ___ cause (2 wds.)
15 Bullets
16 Erase
17 Under no circumstance
18 Actor Sean
19 Partiality
20 Egyptian beetle
22 Actress Vardalos
23 Walk ___ Line
24 Cruel dictator ___ Pot
26 ___, Sawyer County
29 Platter
33 ___ Lake, Burnett County (Ursa Major, 2 wds.)
36 Don't drink it in Mexico?
37 Like the Joker or the Penguin
38 Golfer Woods
42 "Easy ___ it"
43 ___ Fjords National Park, Alaska
45 South of Ecuador
46 First step in refinishing wood
48 Seller's constraints
49 West of Vietnam
50 ___, Richland County
52 Gaelic
53 ___, Washington and Florence Counties

56 Time period
58 Once ___ lifetime (2 wds.)
59 Elegantly dressed man
62 Uses the "In" door
67 Mix
69 Membership fees
71 Poisonous
72 Actress Kudrow
73 ___ Spumante
74 Prefix for a European country
75 Grade school (abbr.)
76 ___ Prairie, Saint Croix County
77 ___ Creek, Waupaca County

Down

1 Teen shoe manufacturer
2 Utility co.
3 Stellar explosion
4 Drug addict
5 Belt
6 Where you will find the themed answers for this puzzle
7 Harbinger
8 Dodge model
9 Where the Streets Have ___ (2 wds.)
10 Massage
11 Bring together
12 Moscow's home state

13 Brown ___
21 Ice skater Nicole ___
25 "___ 11:00" (2 wds.)
27 Munch
28 Play in baseball
29 June honorees
30 ___ You Babe (2 wds.)
31 Litigator
32 Turtle Lake or Potawatomi
34 Knife made famous by TV ads
35 Street magician David
39 Equipment
40 God of love
41 Deceptive maneuver
44 River in France
47 Mile ___ hour
51 Favorite zoo inhabitants
53 Row
54 As far as
55 Pay increase
57 Caper
60 Overthrow
61 Second in importance
63 Dorothy's dog
64 Test
65 Agitate
66 One from the northern UK
68 Animal representing Aries
70 Formal title

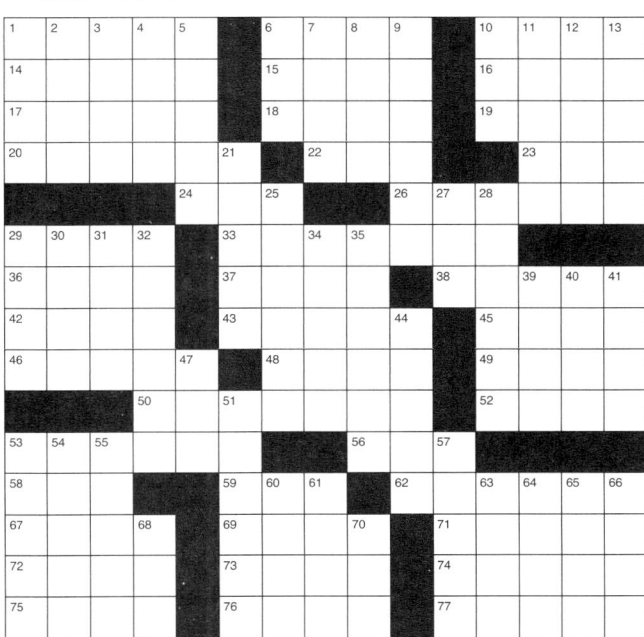

Solution on page 147.

127

Astronaut Quote Game

Put the answer to each clue on the numbered blank. Then transfer the letters into their appropriately numbered spots in the grid above. Work back and forth to solve. When complete, the puzzle will reveal a quote by astronaut Laurel Clark.

1D	2G	3K	■	4M	5F	6G	7F	8N	■	9G	10B	11A	12Q	13O	■	14F	15G	16H	17J
■	18I	■	19P	20L	21D	22N	23M	■	24G	25Q	■	26L	27B	28E	■	29E	30I	31M	32I
33O	34F	35G	36F	37G	38J	■	39H	40B	■	41O	42I	43C	44L	45A	46H	47K	48N	49G	
50G	51I	52L	53N	54P	55C	56F	■	57N	■	58F	59K	60C	61A	■	62D	63P	64J	65G	66C
67A	68Q	69E	70J	71N	■	72B	73D	74C	75Q	■	76G	77B	78E	79F	80E	81C	82G	83B	
84P	85J	■	86F	87B	88M	■	89G	■	90G	91C	92P	93F	94G	95C	96K	97Q	98F	■	99I
100M	101J	102P	103F	■	104H	105A	106G	107D	■	108K	109I	110J	111B	■	112F	113G	114L	115O	116G
117N	118H	■	119D	120L	■	121P	122B	■	123K	124G	125I	126B	127Q	128A	129G	130B	131C	■	132L
133M	134C	■	135B	136H	137Q	138F	139K	140Q	■	141F	142G	143L	144D	145O	146G	147N	148G	149E	
150H	151G	152F	153O	154I	155L														

A __ __ __ __ __ __   Native American tribe
45 128 61 105 67 11

B __ __ __ __ __ __ __ __ __ __ __   Burger side order
40 135 10 122 126 27   72 111 130 77 83

C __ __ __ __ __ __ __ __ __   Imagined
91 74 60 95 43 81 55 131 66 134

D __ __ __ __ __ __ __   John Dillinger had one
107 62 144 21 73 119 1   in Wisconsin

E __ __ __ __ __ __   Northwoods industry
149 29 78 69 28 80

F __ __ __ __ __ __ __ __   The Millionaire on
14 58 93 34 112 87 152 56   *Gilligan's Island*

__ __ __ __ __ __ __ __ __
7 79 141 103 138 98   5 36 86

G __ __ __ __ __ __ __ __ __ __ -   1998 film with a
37 15 151 146 113 129   35 142 76 82   Brett Favre cameo

__ __ __ __ __ __ __ __ __ __ __ __ __ __
106 2 124 49 6   24 90 116 148 94   50 89 65 9

H _ _ _ _ _ _ _ There are six of them in Clue
104 136 16 150 39 46 118

I _ _ _ _ _ _ _ _ _ Fancy outdoor shelters
99 51 32 18 154 42 109 30 125

J _ _ _ _ _ _ _ Teachers
85 101 64 110 70 17 38

K _ _ _ _ _ _ _ Goes back and forth
123 59 96 108 139 3 47

L _ _ _ _ _ _ _ _ _ Took a siesta
44 114 26 143 132 20 120 155 52

M _ _ _ _ _ _ Christmas tree decoration
23 31 133 88 4 100

N _ _ _ _ _ _ _ _ Forever
53 22 147 48 117 57 8 71

O _ _ _ _ _ _ Cleans the floor
13 41 33 145 153 115

P _ _ _ _ _ _ _ Ho-Chunk and Potawatomi
102 92 54 121 63 84 19

Q _ _ _ _ _ _ _ _ Nerve related to hearing
137 97 75 68 25 127 12 140

Solution on page 147.

Across

1 Happy
5 Cole ___
9 Debonair
14 Garden implement
15 Lawyer's suit
16 Wedding attendant
17 "___ they say…" (2 wds.)
18 Destroy
19 Gets closer
20 ___-Cone machine
21 Gave a speech
23 Adios
24 Relating to the sense of touch
27 "The Way" in Chinese
29 Eerie light that hovers over swampy Wisconsin lands at night (4 wds., hyph.)
35 Capital of Vietnam
38 Service charge
39 Great Lake
40 Beer
41 Provide food
43 Bed and breakfast
44 Actress Hatcher
46 We ___ the World
47 Ponders
49 Cursed house in Merrill on Jenny's Hill (2 wds.)
53 Murder, ___ Wrote
54 Fleet's commander in chief

58 Big lump
61 Tire or planet activity
64 Whatever
65 Where Davy Crockett died
67 Inter ___
68 Envelope abbr.
69 Napkin material
70 Hollywood notable Reiner
71 Secular
72 Corner
73 Affiliations
74 Small measure

Down

1 ___ Island in Chippewa Flowage, site of odd mists and noises
2 Actress Luft
3 Org.
4 Gloria in Excelsis ___
5 Ancient parchment
6 Hardy's partner
7 Mongolia's continent
8 Left
9 Ice cream ___
10 Work
11 Melville's Captain
12 Quite
13 Gaelic
22 Archaic anesthetic
25 Duo

26 Three
28 Be in debt
30 Frequently
31 Golf peg
32 Spring bloomer
33 Trigonometry term
34 Cages
35 Ball caps
36 Actor Baldwin
37 Roman Emperor 37-68
41 Brief and notable role
42 Southern constellation
45 Baby ___ Cold Outside
47 Dad's mate
48 One prefix
50 King's chair
51 Witty language
52 Models of perfection
55 Wickerworker sticks (var.)
56 Prank
57 The Richard ___ farmstead in 1870s St. Croix County was the site of famous poltergeist activity
58 Party
59 Actress Lena of Chocolat
60 Pop
62 Consideration
63 Jai ___
66 Singer Torme
68 Boxer Mohammed

130

Solution on page 147.

Read the six spooky snippets that have become legend in different cities in Wisconsin. Then try to match each description to the place where it is credited to have occurred.

A Horicon

1 Every night for a winter a black caped figure walked through West Algoma, which is now part of this city.

B Kenosha

2 Both the Grand Theater and Rogers Theater in this city are the site of hauntings.

C Mineral Point

3 Kemper Hall on the UW campus in this city is said to be haunted by nuns.

D Oshkosh

4 In this city, Walker House, Wisconsin's oldest inn, is haunted by a murderer who was hanged on the premises.

E Rochester

5 This town reportedly had a haunted house in the 1980s, stemming from the purchase of second-hand bunk beds.

F Wausau

6 Chances Restaurant, which was once the Old Union House, is the site of strange happenings.

Solution on page 141.

The following four quotes pertain to our sometimes spooky state. To solve the three cryptoquotes below, you must break the letter substitution code. The code is different for all three puzzles. Follow the directions on the next page to solve the fourth quote.

1 NRXVQPXRP VQPLIRPX UQHC OFQXLX
WCH XAYIHC URBC LFIP IPM XLILC
RP LFC PILRQP.
— Robert Gard, *Wisconsin Lore*

2 HPHKB PYNNXUH XTS AYRB YT QDJRW-
OHQR OYQADTQYT WXQ X UWDQR
QRDKB DK ROD. GJR MDK RWH QWHHK
TJIGHKQ XTS DSS AYKAJIQRXTAHQ
IYTHKXN EDYTR DJRQRKYEQ RWHI XNN.
— Dennis Boyer, *Driftless Spirits*

3 BFCUWBP ZKSU FKC FI CUG FTLWBNTR
UNJJGBV WB UKLVFB ... GOSGJC CUG
AGPGBLNTR DWVWCV QR CUG PUFVC
FI JNVSUNA NALTWSU.
— Michael Norman and Beth Scott,
Haunted Wisconsin

Solution on page 146.

Our Spooky State Quote Game

Put the answer to each clue on the numbered blank. Then transfer the letters into their appropriately numbered spots in the grid above. Work back and forth to solve. When complete, the puzzle will reveal a passage by Jay Rath from *The W-Files*, describing a curious phenomenon that happened off and on throughout July 1970.

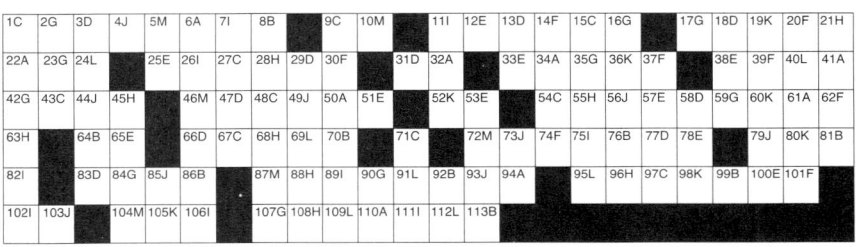

1C	2G	3D	4J	5M	6A	7I	8B		9C	10M		11I	12E	13D	14F	15C	16G		17G	18D	19K	20F	21H
22A	23G	24L		25E	26I	27C	28H	29D	30F		31D	32A		33E	34A	35G	36K	37F		38E	39F	40L	41A
42G	43C	44J	45H		46M	47D	48C	49J	50A	51E		52K	53E		54C	55H	56J	57E	58D	59G	60K	61A	62F
63H		64B	65E		66D	67C	68H	69L	70B		71C		72M	73J	74F	75I	76B	77D	78E		79J	80K	81B
82I		83D	84G	85J	86B		87M	88H	89I	90G	91L	92B	93J	94A		95L	96H	97C	98K	99B	100E	101F
102I	103J		104M	105K	106I		107G	108H	109L	110A	111I	112L	113B

A _ _ _ _ _ _ _ _ _
22 34 32 50 41 6 61 110 94
Cranked

B _ _ _ _ _ _ _ _ _
76 81 92 64 70 99 113 8 86
Canada's ___ Territories

C _ _ _ _ _ _ _ _ _ _
1 48 15 43 71 54 67 97 27 9
A big commotion

D _ _ _ _ _ _ _ _ _ _
66 18 31 47 58 3 77 83 13 29
First US President

E _ _ _ _ _ _ _ _ _ _
38 51 100 33 25 78 57 12 65 53
Color-changing critter

F _ _ _ _ _ _ _ _
74 20 39 14 37 62 30 101
Queen's *Bohemian* ___

G _ _ _ _ _ _ _ _ _ _
17 35 16 90 59 84 42 2 107 23
Atmosphere's warming effect

H _ _ _ _ _ _ _ _ _
88 55 63 45 68 28 96 108 21
Use a comma or an apostrophe

I _ _ _ _ _ _ _   _ _
82 26 75 89 111 106 7   102 11
Engrossed

J _ _ _ _ _ _ _ _ _
103 85 49 73 56 44 4 79 93
Bird in a pear tree

K _ _ _ _ _ _ _
98 80 52 60 105 19 36
Dizzy

L _ _ _ _ _ _ _
112 91 40 69 95 109 24
Locked

M _ _ _ _ _ _
46 5 87 10 104 72
Arts and ___ style of architecture

Solution on page 146.

ANSWERS

Wisconsin County Names Answers

```
F I T S ■ ■ S H O P ■ ■ L A G
L O R E ■ S H O N E ■ E U R O
A W O L ■ T A L O N ■ A R E A
B A Y F I E L D ■ ■ C R E S T
■ ■ ■ N N E ■ S P A T ■ ■ ■ ■
O C O N T O ■ W A U S H A R A
F L A I L ■ S H I R E ■ T O D
F A K E ■ S E I N E ■ S U M O
A R E ■ S P E N T ■ H I R E R
L A N G L A D E ■ V E R N O N
■ ■ A I R Y ■ C I A ■ ■ ■ ■
S H O U T ■ F L O R E N C E
H U N G ■ C O R A L ■ L E A R
E L L E ■ H Y E N A ■ S A R I
D A Y ■ O L E G ■ E R S E
```

Wisconsin City Nicknames Answers

```
S W A B ■ S T O P ■ ■ T A C K
P E R U ■ T A T U M ■ I N R I
E V E R ■ E X T R A ■ E T O N
D E A L E R ■ ■ E T T R I C K
■ ■ I T E R ■ R A H ■ ■ ■
M O N R O E S ■ D E M E A N
S A R G E ■ P A L O ■ A R G O
P R A T ■ D O T E R ■ R A N I
I S T O ■ I T E M ■ A S T E R
T H E N C E ■ S O M E H O W
■ ■ I T S ■ N E R F ■ ■ ■
D E L A V A N ■ R O I L E D
A M E N ■ R E N E E ■ E U R O
B I T E ■ Y A N K S ■ L A I R
S T O W ■ D E E T ■ D U N K
```

Wisconsin County Quick Facts Answers

```
D E E R ■ T A C T ■ P I T C H
O L E O ■ A R O W ■ A W A R E
M I L W A U K E E ■ N O M A D
E S S E N ■ D R A T ■ P I G
■ ■ N I T S ■ P O R T A G E
M A R A T H O N ■ L Y E ■ ■
E R A ■ A I D A N ■ S C A N
L I M E ■ S A V O R ■ T A C O
T A P S ■ S E L I G ■ Y E S
■ ■ A S P ■ L A C R O S S E
O Z A U K E E ■ N E O N ■ ■
R I M ■ A W L S ■ O L E A N
C L O U T ■ M E N O M I N E E
A C U T E ■ E T O N ■ N O O N
S H R E D ■ R I T E ■ E S N E
```

Wisconsin City Code Names Answers

```
A B C S ■ L O E S S ■ A R M S
C O O P ■ E N A C T ■ B E A U
E L L E ■ T E T R A ■ E N O S
D E T E R ■ S U L A ■ E R A
■ ■ D A T A ■ B A L D W I N
M A R S H A L L ■ G A R ■ ■
I D A ■ S C O L D ■ S A L O N
S A N D ■ O H A R A ■ T O R O
T Y K E S ■ A M A S S ■ O S U
■ ■ S P A ■ A P P L E T O N
M U S K E G O ■ E S A U ■ ■
A P T ■ D E N Y ■ P R I M E
S P E W ■ N I E C E ■ E V E R
S E N D ■ D O N E E ■ K E E N
E R O S ■ A N S E L ■ A S K S
```

Wisconsin Cities Answers: 1. Arbor Vitae 2. Ashwaubenon 3. Beaver Dam 4. Blanchardville 5. Boscobel 6. Campbellsport 7. Crivitz 8. Delavan 9. Egg Harbor 10. Germantown 11. Hazel Green 12. Kaukauna 13. Land O'Lakes 14. Maple Bluff 15. Oconomowoc 16. Pardeeville 17. Rice Lake 18. Shawano 19. Waupaca 20. Wisconsin Rapids

Wisconsin Cities A to Z Answers: 1. Algoma 2. Ixonia 3. Beloit 4. Cable 5. Waupun 6. Poynette 7. Medford 8. Cedarburg 9. Chenequa 10. Crandon 11. Tomah 12. Grafton 13. Shawano 14. Oconto 15. Lancaster 16. Mosinee 17. Spooner 18. Ephraim 19. Marinette 20. Wabeno 21. Milton 22. Lomira 23. Sturtevant 24. Nekoosa 25. Wauzeka 26. Juda

Wisconsin Cities Revealed Answers: 1. Kenosha 2. New Glarus 3. Sheboygan 4. Sun Prairie 5. Phillips 6. Stevens Point 7. Superior 8. Sparta 9. Oshkosh 10. Hudson

More Wisconsin Cities Phonetically Answers: 1. La Crosse 2. Colfax 3. Neillsville 4. Adams 5. Princeton 6. Sauk City 7. Eagle 8. Marion 9. Rice Lake 10. Okauchee

Wisconsin Lakes Trivia Answers: 1. Michigan and Superior 2. Devil's Lake 3. Yes (15,081) 4. Green Lake 5. Hill of the Dead 6. Glaciers 7. Mud Lake 8. Rock Lake 9. Vilas

Wisconsin Lakes Revealed Answers: 1. Turtle-Flambeau Flowage 2. Castle Rock Lake 3. Lake Geneva 4. Lake Wissota 5. Lake Winnebago 6. Lake Pepin 7. Lake Mendota 8. Lake Chippewa Flowage 9. Lake Wisconsin 10. Lake Koshkonong

Wisconsin Lakes Answers: 1. Big Bass 2. Butternut 3. Chetek 4. Delton 5. Dutch Hollow 6. Elkhart 7. Half Moon 8. Kegonsa 9. Little St. Germain 10. Metonga 11. Muskellunge 12. Nokomis 13. Pewaukee 14. Presque Isle 15. Puckaway 16. Sinissippi 17. Tomahawk 18. Vermillion 19. Waubesa 20. White Potato

Wisconsin Sports Trivia Answers: 1. Tiger Woods 2. Snowmobile 3. Italian, Polish, Bratwurst, Hot Dog, Chorizo 4. Eric Heiden 5. Wrestling 6. Engine 7. Baseball 8. Bowling alleys 9. Snowshoes

Wisconsin County Fill-In Answers

W	A	L	W	O	R	T	H		C	L	A	R	K		M	A	R	Q	U	E	T	T	E
O		A		R		R			R						A								A
O	Z	A	U	K	E	E		A			M	A	R	I	N	E	T	T	E				U
D		S		M	I	L	W	A	U	K	E	E		A									C
	H		P		F				N		T	A	Y	L	O	R			L
K	E	W	A	U	N	E	E		O	C	O	N	T	O		H		A			L
E		R		A		R		N		M		O		C			A
N			A	S	H	L	A	N	D		E		I		N		R		C		R
O		O		E				I		N		P	O	R	T	A	G	E
S		U		D	A	N	E		D		E		S			L
H		T		U			W	A	U	K	E	S	H	A		S		R	U	S	K
A	D	A	M	S		I	O	W	A				A		E		M
	G				S			W		D		S		E		P
G	R	A	N	T		C	H	I	P	P	E	W	A		T		T
R		M		L		I		O		N		N		R		I
E		I		B	A	R	R	O	N		L	I	N	C	O	L	N		R		C
E		E		F		G		K				R			O
N		V	I	L	A	S		T						P	I	E	R	C	E
	Y		F	O	N	D	D	U	L	A	C		X		O
B	A	Y	F	I	E	L	D		N		O		V		C
U		T		O		D		G	R	E	E	N	L	A	K	E
F	O	R	E	S	T		O		G		M		R
F		E		E	R		S	H	E	B	O	Y	G	A	N		B
A		P		N				N		O		O
F	L	O	R	E	N	C	E		C		R		W	I	N	N	E	B	A	G	O
O		P		R		O		O		W
	I		L	A	N	G	L	A	D	E		J	E	F	F	E	R	S	O	N
W		N		C		U				I
A		I		M	A	N	I	T	O	W	O	C		C
J	U	N	E	A	U		B				H
P		E		I		D	O	U	G	L	A	S
J	A	C	K	S	O	N		S	A	W	Y	E	R		A		A
C					O				N		U
W	A	S	H	B	U	R	N		B	U	R	N	E	T	T		D		K

Wisconsin Counties Revealed: 1. Iron County 2. Richland County 3. Fond du Lac County 4. Juneau County 5. Lafayette County 6. Sauk County 7. Langlade County 8. Calumet County 9. Burnett County 10. Bayfield County

Wisconsin Counties A to Z Answers: 1. Calumet 2. Winnebago 3. Jackson 4. Dodge 5. Oneida 6. Buffalo 7. Outagamie 8. Ashland 9. Racine 10. Juneau 11. Sauk 12. Richland 13. Menominee 14. Kewaunee 15. Monroe 16. Trempealeau 17. Marquette 18. Burnett 19. Washington 20. Manitowoc 21. Washburn 22. Vilas 23. Iowa 24. St. Croix 25. Sheboygan 26. Ozaukee

Wisconsin Cities Phonetically Answers

```
H A L F ■ T W E A K ■ O A R S
O D O R ■ C H A C O ■ P L O T
L A V A ■ M A S E R ■ T I V O
A M E N D ■ ■ T R E E ■ B E N
■ ■ C A L L ■ B A Y S I D E
S U P E R I O R ■ ■ N E W ■
E N E ■ K A B O B ■ S I M O N
E T A L ■ M E T A L ■ M I R E
M O R A L ■ D A T E D ■ L E E
■ ■ N O D ■ S H E R W O O D
B E L G I U M ■ ■ E R I E ■
A L A ■ N E A T ■ P A V E R
Y U R T ■ L U R E S ■ S I Z E
E D G E ■ E V I T A ■ E T R E
R E E D ■ R E P A Y ■ L O A F
```

Wisconsin Winter Sports Answers

```
C R A B ■ A L T A R ■ S T A G
H O Y A ■ D I O N E ■ T O M E
I C E S K A T I N G ■ A B E T
■ H E G E L ■ U N I O N S
P E S ■ A I R ■ S L A N G ■
E L N I N O ■ D E A N ■ G P S
A D O R E ■ R E N T A ■ A R A
H E W S ■ C A N O E ■ S N A G
E S S ■ W A D E R ■ S L I N G
N T H ■ A R A B ■ A T O N C E
■ O T T E R ■ M M R ■ G E D
A L E R T S ■ R A O U L ■
L E I A ■ S K I J U M P I N G
P E N N ■ E L T O N ■ G L U E
O R G S ■ S M A R T ■ A L T O
```

Wisconsin Lakes Answers

```
R E G I S ■ L A R D ■ C E S S
E D I T H ■ O R E O ■ U T A H
B A L S A ■ W I N N E B A G O
A M A ■ W E E D ■ R E L E T
■ P A R R ■ S L I D ■
M O N O N A ■ E P I C ■ A N T
A L A M O ■ L A I R S ■ L E I
L I S P ■ B E R R A ■ T O G A
E V A ■ I R A T E ■ M I N E R
S E L ■ D A S H ■ G E N E V A
■ O A T H ■ H U N T ■
S T A S H ■ L A N D ■ N E D
W I S C O N S I N ■ O C A L A
A R E A ■ I R E D ■ T O T A L
B E A R ■ P O N Y ■ A G O N Y
```

Wisconsin Winter Olympians Answers

```
A D A M ■ S L O T ■ B L A I R
D E L I ■ A O N E ■ U I N T A
D E E D ■ C R E E ■ R E T A R
E R R ■ H E I D E N ■ I L E
R E T A K E N ■ R E D ■
■ F I T Z R A N D O L P H
P A S T A ■ I D S ■ T A L E
U S E ■ C O A S T ■ N I A
N A R Y ■ O A T ■ E A G E R
S P E E D S K A T I N G ■
■ S E T ■ E N D O R S E
D A S ■ J A N S E N ■ O U R
R U N T O ■ A N N A ■ I D E A
A D I E U ■ P O S T ■ L I D S
W I T T Y ■ S T Y E ■ K N E E
```

Wisconsin Winter Sports Trivia Answers: 1. Sled 2. Dan Jansen 3. Cross Country Skiing 4. Auger 5. Snowmobile 6. Granite Peak 7. Tip-up 8. Pettit National Ice Center 9. Stevens Point

Badger Trivia Answers: 1. Field House 2. Fifth quarter 3. Alan Ameche and Ron Dayne 4. 1994, 1999, 2000 5. Football, basketball, ice hockey, volleyball, soccer, cross country, tennis, swimming, wrestling, track and field, golf, softball, rowing 6. They won back-to-back championships 7. Buckingham U. Badger 8. Six (1973, 1977, 1981, 1983, 1990, 2006) 9. 1941

Badgers in the Wisconsin Athletic Hall of Fame Answers: 1. Bob Johnson 2. Chris Steinmetz 3. Chuck Fenske 4. David Schreiner 5. Don Gehrmann 6. Don Kindt 7. Elroy Hirsch 8. George Poage 9. Guy Sundt 10. Harlan Rogers 11. Harold "Bud" Foster 12. Howard Buck 13. Ivan Williamson 14. John Messmer 15. Marlin "Pat" Harder 16. Pat Richter 17. Patrick O'Dea 18. Rollie Williams 19. Thomas Jones 20. Walter Meanwell

Packers Trivia Answers: 1. Lambeau leap 2. Patriots 3. The stockholders 4. Ron Wolf 5. Hutson #4, Canadeo #3, Starr #15, Nitschke #66, White #92 6. Brett Favre (himself) 7. Holmgren Way 8. Curly Lambeau 9. Chiefs

The Green Bay Packers Quiz Answers: All are TRUE

Lake Sudoku Answers

S	I	K	N	A	O	W	M	H
A	H	N	W	K	M	O	S	I
O	M	W	I	S	H	A	N	K
K	W	S	O	I	N	M	H	A
M	**O**	**H**	**A**	**W**	**K**	**S**	**I**	**N**
N	A	I	H	M	S	K	W	O
W	N	M	K	H	A	I	O	S
H	S	A	M	O	I	N	K	W
I	K	O	S	N	W	H	A	M

Curling Sudoku Answers

Y	O	P	L	S	N	D	W	A
L	D	N	W	A	Y	P	S	O
S	A	W	P	O	D	Y	L	N
D	W	S	A	N	L	O	P	Y
P	**L**	**A**	**Y**	**D**	**O**	**W**	**N**	**S**
N	Y	O	S	P	W	L	A	D
O	P	D	N	W	S	A	Y	L
W	N	L	O	Y	A	S	D	P
A	S	Y	D	L	P	N	O	W

Golf Sudoku Answers

T	N	E	O	M	G	B	R	A
M	A	G	B	R	T	E	O	N
R	B	O	A	N	E	M	T	G
A	G	N	E	T	O	R	B	M
B	**E**	**R**	**G**	**A**	**M**	**O**	**N**	**T**
O	T	M	N	B	R	G	A	E
G	M	T	R	O	N	A	E	B
N	O	B	M	E	A	T	G	R
E	R	A	T	G	B	N	M	O

Tornado Sudoku Answers

A	S	M	T	I	Y	H	L	D
I	L	T	H	M	D	Y	S	A
D	H	Y	S	L	A	M	I	T
S	T	H	I	A	L	D	M	Y
L	**A**	**D**	**Y**	**S**	**M**	**I**	**T**	**H**
M	Y	I	D	T	H	S	A	L
T	D	S	L	H	I	A	Y	M
H	M	L	A	Y	S	T	D	I
Y	I	A	M	D	T	L	H	S

Native American Sudoku Answers

E	N	M	T	U	O	S	C	A
S	U	T	E	C	A	N	M	O
O	C	A	N	S	M	E	U	T
C	T	U	A	E	N	M	O	S
M	**A**	**S**	**C**	**O**	**U**	**T**	**E**	**N**
N	O	E	S	M	T	C	A	U
A	S	O	M	N	E	U	T	C
T	M	N	U	A	C	O	S	E
U	E	C	O	T	S	A	N	M

Homebrewed Sudoku Answers

L	N	S	C	U	E	O	R	I
U	E	I	L	O	R	C	S	N
R	C	O	I	S	N	U	E	L
I	S	E	O	R	U	L	N	C
C	**O**	**R**	**N**	**E**	**L**	**I**	**U**	**S**
N	L	U	S	C	I	R	O	E
O	R	C	E	L	S	N	I	U
E	I	L	U	N	O	S	C	R
S	U	N	R	I	C	E	L	O

American Birkebeiner Answers

G	A	L	S	■	S	W	E	A	T	■	A	V	E	R
A	R	I	L	■	T	E	M	P	O	■	M	O	V	E
S	I	L	O	■	E	L	T	O	N	■	I	L	E	S
H	A	Y	W	A	R	D	■	Y	O	G	U	R	T	■
■	■	L	E	S	■	S	W	O	O	N	■	■	■	■
E	S	K	I	M	O	■	W	H	I	Z	■	T	A	P
R	I	O	T	S	■	L	E	A	S	E	■	E	S	A
O	M	R	O	■	M	A	I	N	E	■	L	E	S	S
D	O	T	■	P	A	S	S	E	■	B	E	R	E	T
E	N	E	■	A	R	E	S	■	S	I	E	S	T	A
■	■	L	U	N	A	R	■	O	C	T	■	■	■	■
C	L	O	S	E	T	■	C	H	E	Q	T	E	L	■
H	O	P	E	■	H	E	N	C	E	■	U	R	S	A
O	V	E	R	■	O	D	I	U	M	■	I	A	M	B
W	E	T	S	■	N	O	T	R	E	■	D	Y	E	S

Professional Golf Answers

A	J	A	R	■	S	P	A	S	M	■	T	A	S	K
M	I	N	E	■	T	A	S	T	E	■	E	M	M	A
O	L	D	E	■	S	T	E	I	N	H	A	U	E	R
S	T	Y	L	E	■	A	L	T	O	■	S	A	M	■
■	N	E	V	E	R	■	L	O	T	■	E	R	A	■
R	H	O	D	E	S	I	A	■	R	E	B	■	■	■
O	E	R	■	N	A	O	M	I	■	L	O	W	L	Y
P	A	T	H	■	U	T	I	C	A	■	W	H	I	M
E	T	H	E	R	■	S	N	I	P	S	■	I	N	C
■	■	R	E	P	■	O	N	A	L	A	S	K	A	■
M	O	P	■	L	A	S	■	G	R	A	N	T	■	■
A	N	A	■	A	C	H	E	■	M	E	L	E	E	■
J	E	R	R	Y	K	E	L	L	Y	■	M	I	R	A
O	T	T	O	■	E	A	S	E	D	■	I	N	I	T
R	O	S	E	■	T	R	E	E	S	■	A	G	E	S

Wisconsin Snowmobile Trails Answers

W	I	S	P	■	S	U	M	A	C	■	R	O	M	A
A	G	U	E	■	A	R	E	N	A	■	E	M	I	L
L	O	G	E	■	W	I	L	D	R	I	V	E	R	S
T	R	A	W	L	■	D	E	A	R	■	N	E	O	■
■	■	R	E	E	V	E	■	S	T	O	P	■	■	■
A	G	R	E	E	I	N	G	■	S	N	I	P	E	R
T	R	I	■	K	N	O	R	R	■	S	T	E	L	E
L	O	V	E	■	O	L	E	I	C	■	S	C	A	B
A	V	E	R	S	■	A	E	S	O	P	■	A	T	A
S	E	R	A	P	H	■	D	E	C	A	N	T	E	R
■	■	S	O	A	P	■	R	O	D	E	O	■	■	■
U	F	F	■	R	I	L	E	■	S	A	N	T	A	■
G	R	E	A	T	R	I	V	E	R	■	T	I	E	R
L	E	E	R	■	D	E	I	C	E	■	E	C	R	U
Y	E	L	P	■	O	R	L	O	P	■	R	A	N	G

Great Wisconsin Golf Courses Answers

F	I	S	H	■	F	U	M	E	■	T	E	A	C	H
O	N	C	E	■	I	P	O	D	■	A	T	S	E	A
R	A	R	E	■	E	K	E	D	■	P	A	I	N	T
U	N	O	■	S	E	N	A	T	E	■	A	T	E	■
M	E	D	I	A	T	E	■	A	R	I	■	■	■	■
■	■	T	R	A	P	P	E	R	S	T	U	R	N	■
S	E	N	S	E	■	A	N	D	■	E	S	A	U	■
E	V	A	■	S	A	N	D	Y	■	P	V	T	■	■
R	E	N	O	■	O	D	E	■	R	O	S	E	S	■
B	L	A	C	K	W	O	L	F	R	U	N	■	■	■
■	■	T	O	E	■	R	O	M	A	N	C	E	■	■
E	S	P	■	P	R	E	C	U	T	■	E	R	R	■
C	H	E	A	P	■	T	O	G	O	■	C	H	E	R
T	I	T	H	E	■	R	O	A	R	■	O	R	E	O
O	N	E	A	L	■	E	L	L	S	■	B	U	L	L

Vince Lombardi Quotes Answers:

Scrambled Words: 1. The price of success is hard work, dedication to the job at hand, and the determination that whether we win or lose, we have applied the best of ourselves to the task at hand.

2. We didn't lose the game, we just ran out of time.

3. It's not whether you get knocked down, it's whether you get up.

4. We would accomplish many more things if we did not think of them as impossible.

5. Teamwork is what the Green Bay Packers were all about. They didn't do it for individual glory, they did it because they loved one another.

Cryptoquotes: 1. Winning is not a sometime thing; it's an all time thing. You don't win once in a while, you don't do things right once in a while, you do them right all the time. Winning is habit. Unfortunately, so is losing.

2. If you aren't fired with enthusiasm, you will be fired with enthusiasm.

3. A school without football is in danger of deteriorating into a medieval study hall.

4. The difference between a successful person and others is not a lack of strength, not a lack of knowledge, but a lack of will.

5. People who work together will win, whether it be against complex football defenses or the problems of modern society.

The Green Bay Packers Answers

B	L	O	W		C	E	D	A	R		B	A	B	A
A	U	D	I		U	N	I	T	E		A	L	A	R
L	A	D	S		D	E	A	T	H		D	A	Y	S
M	U	S	E	D		L	I	E	S		M	O	O	
		L	E	E	K		C	A	L	H	O	U	N	
B	I	C	Y	C	L	E	S		T	E	A			
A	N	I		A	M	A	H	S		W	R	A	T	H
S	C	A	N		S	T	E	L	E		D	U	R	A
S	H	O	U	T		S	E	E	T	O		R	A	T
		M	R	S		T	E	A	M	N	A	M	E	
I	C	E	B	O	W	L		P	L	I	E			
T	A	R		T	E	A	K		T	R	E	S	S	
E	R	I	N		A	B	O	V	E		V	A	I	N
M	A	C	E		T	E	N	E	T		E	R	M	A
S	T	A	T		S	L	A	T	E		S	L	I	P

Wisconsin Stock-Car Racing Venues Answers

F	L	O	A	T		C	O	R	A	L		M	I	R
L	A	T	C	H		A	P	E	R	Y		A	R	E
A	D	I	E	U		J	E	F	F	E	R	S	O	N
W	E	S		N	O	U	N	S			I	S	N	T
			E	D	E	N			A	M	P			
S	I	S	T	E	R		O	T	T	O		C	B	S
O	S	C	A	R		G	R	E	E	N		A	L	T
C	L	O	T	H		R	A	T		S	C	R	E	E
K	E	N		I	R	A	T	E		T	O	T	A	L
S	T	E		L	O	B	E		B	E	R	A	T	E
		P	L	Y			T	U	R	N				
T	A	C	O		S	T	A	S	H		G	A	S	
S	T	A	T	E	P	A	R	K		A	D	O	R	E
A	O	L		B	O	G	I	E		L	Y	R	I	C
R	P	M		B	I	S	O	N		L	E	E	D	S

Green Bay Packers Coaches Answers

A	R	A	B		O	D	O	R		I	B	S	E	N
C	O	L	A		R	I	M	E		N	E	O	L	A
E	T	O	N		E	P	I	C		F	A	R	G	O
S	E	E	T	O		T	U	B	A		T	I	M	
		A	L	E	S		R	O	N	Z	A	N	I	
H	O	L	M	G	R	E	N		A	T	E			
A	N	Y		A	S	L	A	P		E	R	U	P	T
I	C	E	S		E	L	S	I	E		O	S	L	O
R	E	S	T	S		S	A	L	S	A		E	O	N
		A	H	A		L	O	M	B	A	R	D	I	
L	A	M	B	E	A	U		T	E	E	N			
I	D	I		R	A	N	K		T	I	T	L	E	
V	E	N	O	M		I	N	S	O		M	O	O	D
E	L	E	N	A		T	E	A	K		A	T	M	E
S	E	D	A	N		E	E	L	S		L	E	A	N

Wisconsin's Need for Speed Answers

W	A	T	T		S	T	R	A	I	T		S	A	G
A	S	I	A		T	W	I	R	L	S		C	U	R
D	I	C	K	T	R	I	C	K	L	E		O	R	E
			E	R	A	T	O				S	T	A	G
S	A	M		I	N	S		S	T	A	R	T		
P	R	A	Y	E	D		B	U	R	R	O	W	E	R
R	A	T	E	D		B	R	I	E	F		I	D	O
A	R	T	S		E	L	I	T	E		E	M	M	A
Y	A	K		I	R	O	N	S		M	E	M	O	S
S	T	E	R	L	I	N	G		T	A	L	E	N	T
		N	A	K	E	D		B	E	G		R	D	S
M	U	S	T			A	R	N	O	T				
E	S	E		T	E	D	M	U	S	G	R	A	V	E
S	E	T		A	D	V	I	C	E		O	D	I	N
A	S	H		N	O	D	D	E	D		D	E	E	D

Alan Kulwicki Quotes Answers:
Scrambled Words:
1. First you learn to drive fast. Next, you learn to drive fast in traffic. Then, you learn how to do it for five hundred miles.
2. If you don't believe you don't belong.

Cryptoquotes:
1. I have a motto: Work to become, not to acquire.
2. I didn't work to win a million dollars, I worked to become Winston Cup Champion.
3. In every aspect of life, have a game plan, and then do your best to achieve it.

Wisconsin State Forests Answers: 1. Black River 2. Brule River 3. Coulee Experimental
4. Flambeau 5. Governor Knowles 6. Havenwoods 7. Kettle Moraine
8. Northern Highland-American Legion 9. Peshtigo River 10. Point Beach

State Park Trivia Answers: 1. Frank Lloyd Wright 2. Devil's Lake 3. Swimming pool
4. Fault 5. Teepee 6. Aztalan State Park 7. Copper Culture State Park 8. Wyalusing
9. Straight Lake State Park

Wisconsin State Park Facts Answers

```
E S T O P ■ T O R A H ■ A L L
A L I B I ■ E B O L A ■ M O I
T U N I C ■ M O N A D N O C K
S E T ■ T A P E S ■ ■ E R I E
■ ■ R O S E ■ ■ O P T ■ ■ ■ ■
S L O U G H ■ D E L E ■ J E B
E A G E R ■ B I D E T ■ U N E
E R I S A ■ I O N ■ R A I S A
R E V ■ P R A D A ■ O C C U R
S S E ■ H O S E ■ A G R E E D
■ ■ E S E ■ ■ ■ P O L E ■ ■ ■
A G R A ■ ■ J E L L Y ■ S C I
Q U A R T Z I T E ■ P L E A T
U M P ■ K A B O B ■ H O R S E
A S T ■ O P E N S ■ S T E A M
```

State Wildlife Areas Answers

```
A C T A ■ T O T E M ■ T I P S
C L O D ■ A R O M A ■ I D E A
M U D D Y C R E E K ■ C L A N
E B O L A ■ ■ D R E ■ H E L D
■ ■ ■ E C R U ■ Y U R I ■ ■ ■
S A N D H I L L ■ P A G A N S
I R E ■ T A C I T ■ H A D I T
T E A K ■ L E T U P ■ N I K E
U N R I G ■ R E N E S ■ E O N
P A S C A L ■ M I S C A U N O
■ ■ ■ K I E V ■ C O O L ■ ■ ■
A B B A ■ S O S ■ ■ U I N T A
L E A P ■ S I L V E R N A I L
T R I O ■ E L O I S ■ E M M A
O T T O ■ N A P E S ■ S E E N
```

Wisconsin State Parks Answers

```
S C A R ■ T E A P O T ■ P R O
E L L A ■ A L M O N D ■ O E R
C O P P E R F A L L S ■ T E A
S P O I L ■ S K Y ■ ■ T A L L
■ ■ E L A N ■ A S K E W ■ ■ ■
H A R R I S O N ■ O A X A C A
O R O ■ S E L E S ■ T A T E R
S E C T ■ A T R I A ■ S O D A
T A K E R ■ E V E N S ■ M E G
A S Y L U M ■ E V E N T I D E
■ ■ A L T E R ■ E W E R ■ ■ ■
S A R S ■ R I A ■ ■ E Y I N G
O R B ■ W I L L O W R I V E R
R I O ■ O N E I D A ■ N A V E
E A R ■ P O S T E R ■ G N A W
```

Wisconsin Weather Answers

```
H A L F ■ J U L Y ■ ■ ■ D D S
E V I L ■ A E R I E ■ B E A U
R O M E ■ P L A N T ■ R A Z E
S N O W F A L L ■ ■ M I N E R
■ ■ ■ I C Y ■ S P A N ■ ■ ■ ■
N A T I V E ■ C O U D E R A Y
O C H R E ■ D A N C E ■ E W E
S U R E ■ B A D G E ■ G L A M
E T E ■ C L U E S ■ L O I R E
D E W P O I N T ■ R O T T E N
■ ■ ■ R A P T ■ G A I ■ ■ ■ ■
A N N A L ■ ■ R A I N F A L L
M E O W ■ H O U R S ■ O L I O
E V A N ■ A S I D E ■ R O S S
S A M ■ ■ J U N E ■ ■ K E P T
```

Wisconsin State Parks Revealed Answers: 1. Rock Island State Park 2. Interstate State Park 3. Kohler-Andrae State Park 4. Devil's Lake State Park 5. Wyalusing State Park 6. Copper Falls State Park 7. Blue Mound State Park 8. Rib Mountain State Park 9. High Cliff State Park 10. Peninsula State Park

Wisconsin State Wildlife Areas Answers: 1. Amsterdam Sloughs 2. Beulah Station 3. Clover Valley 4. Crex Meadows 5. Eau Galle River 6. French Creek 7. Gardner Swamp 8. Horicon Marsh 9. Killsnake 10. Kimberly Clark 11. Lake Noquebay 12. New Munster 13. North Bend Bottoms 14. Pine Island 15. Rome Pond 16. Scuppernong 17. Tom Lawin 18. Totagatic Lake 19. Waterloo 20. Whitman Dam

Wisconsin State Trails Answers: 1. Ahnapee 2. Badger 3. Bearskin 4. Buffalo River 5. Capital City 6. Cattail 7. Eisenbahn 8. Fox River 9. Gandy Dancer 10. Glacial Drumlin 11. Green River 12. Military Ridge 13. Mountain-Bay 14. Old Abe 15. Red Cedar 16. Saunders 17. Tomorrow River 18. Tuscobia 19. Wild Goose 20. Wiouwash

Wisconsin Weather Trivia Answers: 1. January 2. February 3. June 4. Lake-effect snow 5. Ice 6. 1993 7. New Richmond 8. Madison 9. Cobwebs

Haunted Matching Answers: 1D, 2F, 3B, 4C, 5A, 6E

Wisconsin Tornadoes Answers

```
L E A D ■ T A M I ■ ■ C L O D
A R G O ■ O P E R A ■ R O V E
M I R O ■ N O O K S ■ I D E A
B E A R D S ■ W E S T B E N D
■ ■ ■ C A I N ■ D U E ■ ■
■ N O O D L E S ■ M A R C H E
M O R U S ■ P A L E ■ O R A L
A K I N ■ L A T E R ■ C E L L
R I O T ■ E L E C ■ S K A T E
C A N Y O N ■ S H T I C K S ■
■ ■ ■ B I G ■ E R G O ■ ■
O A K F I E L D ■ U N U S E D
A C N E ■ N A O M I ■ N E V E
T R E E ■ T R O I S ■ T R I P
H E E L ■ E L A M ■ Y E L P
```

Wisconsin Lighthouses Answers

```
S H O W ■ M E A N T ■ F E E L
P I P E ■ O X B O W ■ L A T E
A L E E ■ D I E G O ■ A G R A
R O C K W E L L ■ R A I L E D
■ ■ ■ A L E ■ L I ■ T R E ■
S E C T S ■ P A V E ■ B V D
C L A W ■ W A R R E N ■ L I E
A T N O ■ I N O U R ■ M U T E
L O A ■ G N O M E S ■ A F A R
A N I ■ O D D S ■ R I F L E
■ ■ S L O P E ■ W O E ■ ■
D E L A N O ■ L A P O I N T E
A L A S ■ I R A T E ■ D I O N
M I N T ■ N E V E R ■ O L E O
P A D S ■ T I A R A ■ L E S S
```

Wisconsin Waterfalls Answers

```
B A R K ■ C A L I F ■ A B L E
A N O N ■ A L A M O ■ B R O W
E T T E ■ R I C A N ■ H O S E
R I C E L A K E ■ F L O W E R
■ ■ ■ A T E ■ L E A R N ■ ■
D E B U T S ■ P A R R ■ S A P
A R I S E ■ A R M E D ■ T W O
I N G E ■ S L E E K ■ L O F T
R I M ■ M U T E D ■ D O N U T
Y E A ■ O P E N ■ B A G E L S
■ ■ N A D E R ■ E A R ■ ■
P R I M E R ■ S I S K I W I T
I O T A ■ I M A G E ■ R I D E
L A O S ■ O A T H S ■ I T E R
E M U S ■ R H E T T ■ S H A M
```

Apostle Islands Answers

```
S P A R ■ C R E W ■ R O W
L A V A ■ L A U R A ■ R E N O
I R E S ■ I C I N G ■ E D E N
M I C H I G A N ■ S N O R T
■ ■ ■ R H O ■ T H E E ■ ■
H E R M I T ■ I R O N W O O D
A L O S S ■ B R U N T ■ M N O
M E D S ■ D O W S E ■ G A E L
A C E ■ O A S I S ■ T O N A L
S T O C K T O N ■ D E V I L S
■ ■ I R A N ■ M I A ■ ■
P A N D A ■ B A S S W O O D
E P E E ■ R E L I C ■ A W A Y
L E A R ■ A L A M O ■ R I F E
E R R ■ D I B S ■ N E S S
```

Wisconsin Environmental Quote Game Answers:

John Muir: A. Steeper B. Whippoorwill C. Groundhog D. Hindsight E. Meningitis F. Uneventful G. Westinghouse H. Yesteryears I. Nickelodeon J. Britannia K. Hurrying L. Withers M. Phenomena N. Viewers O. Pewter P. Musty Q. Swathes. Quote: "Oh, that glorious Wisconsin wilderness! Everything new and pure in the very prime of the spring when Nature's pulses were beating highest and mysteriously keeping time with our own!"

Frank Lloyd Wright: A. Green B. Invitation C. Billy D. Peeled E. Louis Quote: "I believe in God, only I spell it Nature."

Aldo Leopold: A. Manhandles B. Rhinelander C. Abductions D. Shenanigans E. Zoology F. Jubilant G. Effervesces H. Anesthesia I. Paramedic J. Memnon K. Aerates L. Inlay M. Anonymous Quote: "In June as many as a dozen species may burst their buds on a single day. No man can heed all of these anniversaries; no man can ignore all of them."

Apostle Islands Trivia Answers: 1. Bayfield 2. An archipelago 3. Devil's Island 4. Gaylord Nelson 5. Madeline Island 6. Shipwrecks 7. Precambrian 8. Record low lake levels 9. Tombolo

Wisconsin History Trivia Answers: 1. 30th 2. It was untouched by advancing glaciers during the ice ages. 3. Milwaukee 4. It gave women the right to vote. 5. Badgers 6. Fur 7. German POWs 8. Theodore Roosevelt 9. China

Apostle Island Facts Answers

F	I	B	S	■	R	O	M	E	O	■	A	S	I	S
A	L	O	E	■	E	B	E	R	T	■	B	E	N	T
B	L	A	C	K	B	E	A	R	S	■	L	A	C	Y
■	■	■	T	O	A	S	T	■	■	R	E	L	A	X
E	R	S	■	R	T	E	■	L	A	U	R	A	■	
T	E	E	P	E	E	■	P	I	L	E	■	M	O	M
C	L	A	R	A	■	P	A	G	E	D	■	P	M	I
H	I	K	E	■	T	O	T	H	E	■	A	R	E	S
E	S	A	■	M	O	I	S	T	■	S	T	E	L	E
S	H	Y	■	E	E	N	Y	■	P	L	A	Y	E	R
■	A	N	G	S	T	■	B	R	A	■	S	T	Y	
B	A	K	E	S	■	■	D	O	O	M	S	■		
I	R	I	S	■	B	R	O	W	N	S	T	O	N	E
L	E	N	T	■	U	N	L	I	T	■	A	W	O	L
L	A	G	S	■	M	A	T	E	O	■	R	E	D	S

Explorers in Wisconsin Answers

F	R	E	E	S	■	E	G	G	S	■	A	R	K	S
A	O	R	T	A	■	N	O	E	L	■	R	U	N	T
T	H	I	E	F	■	E	U	R	O	■	O	R	E	O
S	E	E	S	A	W	■	T	A	G	■	M	A	L	L
■	■	R	H	O	■	L	A	S	A	L	L	E		
J	O	L	L	I	E	T	■	D	N	A	■	■		
A	S	I	A	■	A	T	E	■	T	H	O	N	G	
I	L	L	S	■	T	O	A	D	S	■	A	P	E	R
L	O	O	S	E	■	R	A	P	■	L	A	N	I	
■	■	A	L	A	■	N	I	C	O	L	E	T		
A	L	L	O	U	E	Z	■	E	E	L	■	■		
B	E	A	M	■	G	A	B	■	S	I	L	V	A	N
B	A	K	E	■	E	L	A	N	■	M	O	O	L	A
O	V	E	N	■	N	E	R	O	■	B	R	I	A	N
T	E	S	S	■	D	A	N	G	■	S	E	D	N	A

Preserving History Answers

N	I	A	S	■	T	E	N	S	■	R	A	C	E	D
E	R	I	E	■	A	M	O	K	■	A	D	O	R	E
W	A	D	E	H	O	U	S	E	■	M	E	R	I	T
T	E	A	S	E	■	E	W	E	S	■	A	C	E	
■	A	R	E	A	■	S	T	E	L	L	A	R		
O	L	D	W	O	R	L	D	■	A	S	I	■		
P	O	E	■	D	O	D	O	S	■	R	A	S	P	
N	E	R	D	■	R	I	M	E	S	■	T	I	L	
■	E	B	B	■	C	A	M	P	F	I	V	E		
P	E	O	N	I	E	S	■	C	O	I	L	■		
A	R	B	■	S	T	U	D	■	N	I	E	C	E	
I	N	E	P	T	■	P	E	N	D	A	R	V	I	S
R	I	S	E	R	■	E	L	O	I	■	T	E	A	S
S	E	E	T	O	■	R	I	N	D	■	S	L	O	E

Wisconsin Inventors Answers

P	O	S	I	T	■	S	O	A	P	■	W	H	A	T
A	N	I	T	A	■	U	R	S	A	■	H	O	L	A
U	T	T	E	R	■	S	C	H	L	O	E	M	E	R
L	O	S	■	H	A	H	A	■	T	R	E	E	S	
■	S	E	M	I	■	P	E	T	E	■				
H	A	R	L	E	Y	■	T	A	K	E	■	D	I	M
I	D	E	A	L	■	L	O	N	E	R	■	A	N	A
D	O	N	T	■	R	I	G	I	D	■	B	R	A	T
E	R	E	■	S	U	M	A	C	■	S	E	I	N	E
S	E	W	■	I	B	I	S	■	W	A	R	N	E	R
■	F	R	E	T	■	S	H	U	N	■				
A	I	S	L	E	■	S	A	Y	S	■	A	R	C	
S	T	E	E	N	B	O	C	K	■	A	T	S	E	A
A	C	N	E	■	A	L	O	E	■	G	A	T	E	S
P	H	D	S	■	G	E	T	S	■	E	C	O	L	E

Great Dates Answers: 1H, 2K, 3N, 4A, 5I, 6L, 7C, 8Q, 9E, 10J, 11G, 12B, 13O, 14D, 15R, 16F, 17P, 18M

Wisconsin's Dark Days Trivia Answers: 1. Ed Gein and Jeffrey Dahmer 2. Peshtigo
3. Sterling Hall 4. Hunting party 5. Miller Park 6. Fog 7. Milk 8. A tiny schooner named
Augusta 9. The council chamber of the territorial legislature

Wisconsin State Symbols Trivia Answers: 1. Robin 2. Polka 3. *On Wisconsin*
4. Sugar maple 5. Forward 6. Wood violet 7. Galena 8. Antigo silt loam 9. Trilobite

The Wisconsin State Seal Answers: 1. Anchor 2. Arm and hammer 3. Badger
4. Bars of lead 5. Coil of rope 6. Cornucopia 7. *E pluribus unum* 8. Forward 9. Miner
10. Pick and shovel 11. Plow 12. Sailor 13. Shield 14. Thirteen stars

Native Americans in Wisconsin Trivia Answers: 1. White buffalo 2. Spearfishing
3. Milwaukee 4. Ho-Chunk 5. Abraham Lincoln and Zachary Taylor 6. Bad River Indian
Reservation 7. Ojibwe 8. Fort Atkinson 9. Waukon Decorah

Chief Black Hawk Quote Game Answers: A. Wolverine B. Pennsylvania C. Butterfly D.
Kickstand E. Uprooted F. Housewife G. Disclosure H. Modify I. Memory J. Mateo K. Widow
L. Hypocrites   Quote: "Rock River was beautiful country. I loved my towns, my cornfields, and
the home of my people. It is yours now. Keep it as we did."

Wisconsin's Oldest Answers

C	A	F	E	■	A	R	E	T	E	■	M	A	R	E
O	U	R	S	■	L	O	G	A	N	■	A	M	I	D
O	R	E	S	■	L	I	G	H	T	H	O	U	S	E
L	A	Y	E	R	■	■	S	O	R	E	■	S	E	N
■	S	N	O	B	S	■	E	E	E	■	E	S	S	
A	N	T	E	L	O	P	E	■	■	E	L	I	■	
T	E	A	■	E	A	R	N	S	■	S	N	I	P	E
O	R	T	S	■	S	A	U	L	T	■	S	C	O	W
M	O	T	O	R	■	T	R	I	E	D	■	E	N	E
■	Y	I	N	■	E	M	E	R	A	L	D	S		
L	A	S	■	V	A	N	■	E	N	O	L	A	■	
A	R	A	■	E	T	O	N	■	P	I	N	T	S	
C	O	U	R	T	H	O	U	S	E	■	E	D	I	T
E	S	T	E	■	A	S	N	E	R	■	N	I	N	E
S	E	E	D	■	N	E	S	T	S	■	S	C	A	M

Wisconsin "Firsts" Answers

A	L	D	O	■	F	L	E	C	K	■	A	Q	U	A
M	O	O	D	■	R	O	M	A	N	■	C	U	R	B
A	U	T	O	M	O	B	I	L	E	■	R	I	G	A
■	■	M	A	N	E	T	■	E	V	E	N	E	D	
D	E	F	E	N	D	S	■	W	H	I	S	T	■	
E	M	O	T	E	S	■	E	R	I	N	■	U	M	A
A	P	R	E	S	■	S	T	A	G	E	■	P	O	M
T	I	E	R	■	P	L	A	T	H	■	P	L	O	P
H	R	S	■	S	O	U	T	H	■	D	E	E	R	E
S	E	T	■	U	T	E	S	■	L	A	T	T	E	R
■	F	L	E	A	S	■	F	I	N	E	S	S	E	
D	R	I	E	S	T	■	A	L	T	E	R	■	■	
E	A	R	N	■	O	U	T	E	R	S	P	A	C	E
A	G	E	D	■	E	S	T	E	E	■	A	V	O	N
L	E	S	S	■	S	E	A	T	S	■	N	A	P	E

Wisconsin Public Indian Mounds Answers

A	B	L	E	■	L	I	L	A	C	■	S	P	E	C
C	O	A	X	■	A	M	A	N	A	■	A	S	E	A
E	A	C	H	■	S	P	I	T	E	■	W	A	R	D
D	R	E	A	M	■	D	I	S	C	■	L	I	E	
■	L	A	D	S	■	C	A	L	U	M	E	T		
R	I	C	E	L	A	K	E	■	R	A	T	■		
A	S	H	■	T	I	E	R	S	■	M	A	R	S	H
C	L	O	D	■	S	W	E	A	T	■	H	I	L	O
K	E	Y	E	S	■	S	C	R	A	P	■	T	A	C
■	A	T	E	■	T	O	M	A	H	A	W	K		
H	O	R	N	U	N	G	■	S	E	R	E	■		
A	P	E	■	N	A	I	L	■	K	A	P	U	T	
T	R	E	E	■	B	L	E	A	K	■	D	U	P	E
E	A	S	T	■	L	L	A	M	A	■	E	C	O	N
S	H	E	A	■	E	S	S	A	Y	■	D	E	N	S

Wisconsin on the Cutting Edge Answers

Z	E	A	L	■	A	W	L	S	■	S	P	O	T	
E	S	S	O	■	E	I	E	I	O	■	C	O	V	E
U	N	T	O	■	G	E	N	R	E	■	E	W	E	S
S	E	A	T	B	E	L	T	■	D	I	N	E	R	S
■	■	L	A	D	■	M	I	T	E	R	■	■		
C	A	N	N	O	N	■	C	A	P	E	■	P	A	Y
O	W	I	N	G	■	S	E	R	U	M	■	L	E	O
M	A	N	E	■	B	O	R	I	S	■	H	A	R	K
A	R	E	■	H	I	R	E	S	■	G	E	N	I	E
S	E	T	■	A	P	E	S	■	W	A	N	T	E	D
■	E	U	R	O	S	■	P	A	S	■	■			
D	I	E	S	E	L	■	H	I	G	H	W	A	Y	S
E	T	N	A	■	A	B	O	V	E	■	I	G	E	T
A	S	T	I	■	R	U	L	E	R	■	P	E	T	E
L	A	H	R	■	D	E	N	S	■	E	D	I	T	

Past and Present Indian Tribes in Wisconsin Answers: 1. Cheyenne 2. Chippewa 3. Dakota 4. Fox 5. Ho-Chunk 6. Housatonic 7. Iroquois 8. Kickapoo 9. Menominee 10. Munsee 11. Noquet 12. Ojibwe 13. Oneida 14. Ottawa 15. Potawatomi 16. Sauk 17. Stockbridges 18. Tionontati 19. Winnebago 20. Wyandot

Another Wisconsin First Answers: Kenosha, Lambeau, Snowmobiling, Milwaukee, Liberace, *Happy Days*, Winnebago, Progressive, Spaniel, Water parks, Mitchell, Monona, Lands' End, Marquette, Uecker, Menominee, Bubbler, Smokey Bear Costume

Capitol Trivia Answers: 1. Rotunda 2. '90s 3. Concerts on the Square 4. Fire 5. Belmont 6. Granite 7. Badger 8. Sixth 9. Emanuel Philipp in 1917

Wisconsin Government Trivia Answers: 1. Joseph McCarthy 2. Republican 3. Seat belts 4. 8 5. Progressive 6. He died of a heart attack a month before he was to take office. 7. 99 8. Drowned 9. Jim Doyle

Beer & Brewing Trivia Answers: 1. Germans 2. .08 3. Lager 4. Schlitz, Pabst, Blatz, Miller 5. Leinenkugel's 6. La Crosse 7. Hodag 8. UW Platteville 9. Walworth

Wisconsin State Capitol Facts Answers

A	R	A	B		C	A	D	S		G	L	O	B	E
N	A	V	E		A	C	R	E		A	E	G	I	S
I	V	A	N		T	H	A	W		R	E	R	A	N
T	E	N		S	I	G	N	A	L		E	S	E	
A	N	T	I	Q	U	E			R	I	M			
			S	U	P	R	E	M	E	C	O	U	R	T
C	A	N	T	O		E	O	N		O	B	O	E	
A	L	I		V	O	L	T	A		E	S	A		
S	E	N	D		E	R	E		A	U	R	A	L	
H	E	A	R	I	N	G	R	O	O	M	S			
		Y	O	U		R	I	P	E	N	E	D		
R	E	F		D	E	N	I	A	L		A	D	E	
A	D	L	A	I		A	N	T	E		R	I	S	E
K	N	O	W	N		I	C	E	R		E	V	E	R
E	A	G	L	E		L	A	D	S		D	E	L	E

Wisconsin's Strange Laws Answers

O	L	S	E	N		A	P	S	E		G	R	A	B
B	A	N	T	U		S	E	A	M		L	A	N	E
I	S	A	A	C		T	A	T	T	O	O	I	N	G
E	S	P		L	E	E	K		B	A	L	E	S	
		D	E	A	R		P	O	E	T				
R	E	P	E	A	T		F	A	D	S		A	N	T
O	I	L	E	R		C	A	N	O	E		D	O	W
A	D	A	M		S	O	B	E	R		C	U	R	E
L	E	T		S	H	A	L	L		F	A	L	S	E
D	R	E		P	O	S	E		L	I	S	T	E	D
		D	I	E	T		H	I	R	E				
R	I	S	E	R			P	I	P	E		A	S	H
U	N	C	L	O	T	H	E	D		M	O	V	I	E
S	T	A	T		W	O	R	E		A	N	I	T	A
S	O	D	A		O	P	T	S		N	E	V	E	R

Wisconsin Governors Answers

S	T	E	E	R		C	L	A	W		B	A	I	T
A	O	R	T	A		H	U	L	A		A	L	T	O
S	U	S	A	N		E	L	I	S		L	E	A	N
S	T	E		D	I	A	L		H	A	S	S	L	E
		A	A	R	P		A	B	B	A				
D	A	N	G	L	E		S	H	U	E		L	S	D
O	R	I	E	L		C	H	A	R	D		O	N	E
Y	A	K	S		T	H	O	R	N		G	R	E	W
L	I	E		A	H	E	A	D		D	O	N	E	E
E	L	S		C	O	S	T		O	R	N	E	R	Y
		A	R	M	S		T	R	E	E				
A	S	L	E	E	P		P	R	E	Y		W	A	S
V	E	E	S		S	T	A	Y		F	E	A	S	T
O	L	I	O		O	O	P	S		U	N	T	I	E
W	A	S	P		N	E	A	T		S	E	T	A	T

Wisconsin Breweries Answers

C	O	M	I	C		E	L	S	E		B	U	L	L
A	G	O	R	A		P	E	O	N		A	S	I	A
S	L	E	E	P		S	A	N	D	C	R	E	E	K
H	E	N		I	R	O	N		H	O	R	D	E	
		A	T	O	M		S	P	A	N				
L	O	G	J	A	M		H	E	R	O		S	P	A
A	U	R	A	L		M	I	D	A	S		N	O	B
S	T	A	R		M	A	D	A	M		P	A	I	L
T	D	S		S	I	R	E	N		N	O	I	S	E
S	O	S		H	E	R	S		M	I	L	L	E	R
		M	A	N	Y		B	E	C	K				
E	A	T	E	R		S	I	L	O		T	O	O	
T	W	I	N	P	O	R	T	S		L	E	A	R	N
A	R	E	S		T	H	E	O		E	M	C	E	E
L	Y	R	A		T	O	W	N		T	U	T	O	R

Political Quotes Answers:

Matching: 1. Jim Doyle 2. Robert M. La Follette 3. Herb Kohl 4. Scott McCallum
5. Russ Feingold 6. Tommy Thompson 7. Gaylord Nelson

1. As I've often said, Wisconsin's greatest strength continues to be the dedicated, hardworking people of our state. They go to work every day, pay their taxes, and raise their kids with good, Midwestern values. – Jim Doyle

2. There's a lot of stress involved when your house is underwater. – Scott McCallum, in a flooded Prairie du Chien

3. The ultimate test of man's conscience may be his willingness to sacrifice something today for future generations whose words of thanks will not be heard. – Gaylord Nelson

4. For the life of me, I cannot understand why the terrorists have not attacked our food supply because it is so easy to do. – Tommy Thompson

5. Americans want to defeat terrorism and they want the basic character of this country to survive and prosper. They want both security and liberty, and unless we give them both – and we can if we try – we have failed. – Russ Feingold

More Strange Laws Answers: 1O, 2D, 3K, 4F, 5I, 6M, 7A, 8G, 9L, 10N, 11H, 12C, 13J, 14B, 15E

La Crosse's Oktoberfest Answers

T	A	M	S	■	C	H	A	I	R	■	F	R	O	M
O	R	A	L	■	S	M	I	T	E	■	R	I	C	O
R	I	P	E	■	T	O	R	C	H	L	I	G	H	T
I	D	L	E	R	■	■	S	H	E	A	■	I	R	E
■	■	E	T	H	I	C	■	Y	A	Y	■	D	E	S
P	I	L	S	E	N	E	R	■	■	T	U	B	■	■
E	N	E	■	A	C	R	E	S	■	P	O	G	O	S
A	F	A	R	■	H	E	L	I	O	■	B	O	R	N
S	O	F	A	S	■	S	I	G	M	A	■	L	E	A
■	■	P	E	R	■	■	C	H	I	L	I	D	O	G
S	A	M	■	R	E	D	■	S	T	A	G	E	■	■
O	R	A	■	U	F	O	S	■	■	I	N	N	E	R
F	E	S	T	M	A	S	T	E	R	■	O	K	L	A
A	N	O	N	■	C	E	A	S	E	■	R	E	M	Y
R	A	N	T	■	E	S	T	E	S	■	E	G	O	S

Hollywood Bigwigs from Wisconsin Answers

W	E	L	T	■	N	I	P	P	E	D	■	M	A	D
H	A	I	R	■	E	D	U	A	R	D	■	A	C	E
O	R	S	O	N	W	E	L	L	E	S	■	T	H	E
■	■	■	T	O	T	A	L	■	■	■	A	H	E	M
E	M	S	■	S	O	L	■	J	A	I	L	■	■	■
A	I	T	K	E	N	■	C	O	N	T	E	S	S	A
S	C	R	O	D	■	B	O	L	T	S	■	H	A	L
E	R	O	S	■	O	L	L	I	E	■	T	A	C	T
L	O	B	■	S	P	A	D	E	■	P	A	C	H	A
S	N	E	A	K	E	R	S	■	Z	U	C	K	E	R
■	■	W	I	N	E	■	M	A	R	■	■	S	T	S
F	I	V	E	■	■	G	A	P	E	S	■	■	■	■
U	N	I	■	C	A	R	L	L	A	E	M	M	L	E
S	A	L	■	A	R	N	E	T	T	■	O	B	E	Y
E	N	E	■	T	E	R	E	S	A	■	G	A	T	E

From Wisconsin to Hollywood Answers

E	M	M	A	■	M	O	O	S	■	N	E	A	R	S
L	E	A	S	■	M	A	L	T	■	O	R	N	O	T
M	A	C	M	U	R	R	A	Y	■	U	N	I	T	E
O	L	E	A	N	■	■	F	L	O	G	■	S	O	W
■	■	■	R	I	P	A	■	E	R	A	S	E	R	S
W	H	I	T	F	O	R	D	■	■	E	T	A	■	■
A	I	R	■	Y	E	S	E	S	■	■	S	H	E	S
S	K	I	M	■	M	O	L	A	R	■	H	O	S	T
P	E	S	O	■	N	I	S	E	I	■	■	B	A	A
■	■	L	A	P	■	■	S	H	A	L	H	O	U	B
C	A	M	E	L	O	T	■	A	R	I	A	■	■	■
A	L	A	■	I	P	O	D	■	■	U	R	A	L	S
J	O	R	G	E	■	K	A	C	Z	M	A	R	E	K
U	N	I	O	N	■	E	L	I	A	■	S	O	D	A
N	E	E	D	S	■	N	E	A	P	■	S	N	A	G

Movies Filmed in Wisconsin Answers

O	T	I	S	■	S	P	A	T	S	■	A	S	A	P
D	A	R	N	■	T	A	R	O	T	■	L	I	L	O
O	R	E	O	■	A	S	T	E	R	■	O	M	A	R
R	E	D	B	E	T	S	Y	■	A	S	H	P	I	T
■	■	■	T	E	E	■	V	I	T	A	L	■	■	■
A	T	H	E	N	S	■	L	O	G	E	■	E	S	P
B	I	O	T	A	■	E	I	G	H	T	■	P	H	I
O	B	O	E	■	I	N	P	U	T	■	F	L	A	N
R	I	P	■	A	R	T	I	E	■	L	E	A	V	E
T	A	D	■	L	O	R	D	■	C	A	N	N	E	S
■	■	R	A	I	N	Y	■	J	A	R	■	■	■	■
S	E	E	S	A	W	■	F	O	R	K	E	E	P	S
E	R	A	S	■	I	L	I	K	E	■	T	R	U	E
L	I	M	E	■	L	I	N	E	S	■	R	O	L	E
L	E	S	T	■	L	E	E	R	S	■	E	S	P	N

Food from Wisconsin Answers: 1. Beef 2. Bratwurst 3. Butter 4. Cheese 5. Cherries 6. Corn 7. Cranberries 8. Eggs 9. Ginseng 10. Honey 11. Ice cream 12. Maple syrup 13. Milk 14. Potatoes 15. Sausage 16. Soy beans 17. Trout 18. Turkey 19. Walleye 20. Wild rice

Food & Fun Trivia Answers: 1. Ketchup museum 2. Limburger 3. Fish boils 4. Ice cream sundae 5. Malted milk and malted milk balls 6. Culver's 7. Yellow 8. Brandy 9. Pickle

The Acting Bug Bites Wisconsin Answers: 1N, 2G, 3I, 4D, 5J, 6E, 7M, 8L, 9H, 10A, 11K, 12F, 13C, 14B

Our Spooky State Answers: 1. Wisconsin contains more ghosts per square mile than any state in the nation. 2. Every village and city in southwest Wisconsin has a ghost story or two; but for the sheer numbers and odd circumstances Mineral Point outstrips them all. 3. Nothing much out of the ordinary happens in Hudson ... except the legendary visits by the ghost of Paschal Aldrich.

Our Spooky State Quote Game Answers: A. Ratcheted B. Northwest C. Hullabaloo D. Washington E. Chamaeleon F. Rhapsody G. Greenhouse H. Punctuate I. Wrapped up J. Partridge K. Flighty L. Latched M. Crafts Quote: "Hundreds of people gathered around St. Mary's Catholic Church in Burlington to watch a strange glow that appeared halfway up the steeple."

Magazines Published in Wisconsin Answers

L	I	A	M	■	F	A	R	M	■	P	O	S	E	D
E	T	N	A	■	A	G	U	A	■	I	N	T	E	R
A	S	T	R	O	N	O	M	Y	■	L	E	E	R	Y
H	A	I	K	U	■	■	P	O	L	L	■	N	I	A
■	■	■	E	N	T	O	■	R	E	A	C	T	E	D
P	O	S	T	C	A	R	D	■	E	R	A	■	■	■
A	L	L	■	E	R	R	O	R	■	■	S	T	A	G
S	A	U	L	■	S	I	R	I	S	■	K	I	L	N
T	Y	R	A	■	■	N	I	G	E	L	■	K	O	A
■	■	■	N	O	R	■	A	G	R	I	V	I	E	W
D	I	A	G	R	A	M	■	S	A	L	E	■	■	■
E	N	D	■	I	D	E	A	■	■	A	R	I	S	E
A	D	O	B	E	■	D	R	U	M	C	O	R	P	S
R	I	P	E	N	■	A	L	M	A	■	N	E	A	T
S	E	T	A	T	■	L	O	P	E	■	A	D	Z	E

Wisconsin Is Out of This World Answers

V	E	N	U	S	■	M	O	O	N	■	R	U	I	N
A	L	O	S	T	■	A	M	M	O	■	U	N	D	O
N	E	V	E	R	■	P	E	N	N	■	B	I	A	S
S	C	A	R	A	B	■	N	I	A	■	■	T	H	E
■	■	■	■	P	O	L	■	M	E	T	E	O	R	
D	I	S	C	■	B	I	G	B	E	A	R	■	■	■
A	G	U	A	■	E	V	I	L	■	T	I	G	E	R
D	O	E	S	■	K	E	N	A	I	■	P	E	R	U
S	T	R	I	P	■	A	S	I	S	■	L	A	O	S
■	■	N	E	P	T	U	N	E	■	E	R	S	E	
A	U	R	O	R	A	■	E	R	A	■	■	■		
I	N	A	■	N	O	B	■	E	N	T	E	R	S	
S	T	I	R	■	D	U	E	S	■	T	O	X	I	C
L	I	S	A	■	A	S	T	I	■	I	T	A	L	O
E	L	E	M	■	S	T	A	R	■	C	O	M	E	T

Wisconsin Astronauts Answers

N	A	T	A	L	■	C	H	E	S	S	■	Y	E	W
E	N	O	L	A	■	A	E	R	I	E	■	E	L	I
S	N	A	F	U	■	J	W	I	L	L	I	A	M	S
T	A	D	■	R	O	U	S	E	■	C	R	O	P	
■	■	W	E	A	N	■	■	O	D	E	■	■		
B	A	S	A	L	T	■	A	G	U	E	■	T	C	M
A	N	T	I	C	■	S	T	A	R	K	■	I	R	E
S	W	I	L	L	■	T	O	P	■	E	S	T	E	S
T	A	N	■	A	L	O	N	E	■	S	O	U	S	A
E	R	G	■	R	I	P	E	■	B	L	A	S	T	S
■	■	E	K	E	■	■	H	E	A	P	■	■		
A	L	O	E	■	S	E	E	D	Y	■	U	T	E	
J	I	M	L	O	V	E	L	L	■	T	E	N	O	R
A	R	E	■	R	I	N	S	E	■	O	G	D	E	N
R	A	N	■	E	A	T	E	N	■	N	O	O	S	E

Wisconsin's Haunted Places Answers

G	L	A	D	■	S	L	A	W	■	S	U	A	V	E
H	O	S	E	■	C	A	S	E	■	U	S	H	E	R
O	R	S	O	■	R	U	I	N	■	N	E	A	R	S
S	N	O	■	O	R	A	T	E	D	■	B	Y	E	
T	A	C	T	I	L	E	■	T	A	O	■	■		
■	■	W	I	L	L	O	T	H	E	W	I	S	P	
H	A	N	O	I	■	F	E	E	■	E	R	I	E	
A	L	E	■	C	A	T	E	R	■	I	N	N		
T	E	R	I	■	A	R	E	■	M	U	S	E	S	
S	C	O	T	T	M	A	N	S	I	O	N	■	■	
■	■	S	H	E	■	A	D	M	I	R	A	L		
G	O	B	■	R	O	T	A	T	E	■	A	N	Y	
A	L	A	M	O	■	A	L	I	A	■	A	T	T	N
L	I	N	E	N	■	C	A	R	L	■	L	A	I	C
A	N	G	L	E	■	T	I	E	S	■	I	N	C	H

TV Shows Set in Wisconsin Trivia Answers: 1. *Happy Days* 2. *Laverne and Shirley* 3. *That 70s Show* 4. *Picket Fences* 5. *The Young and the Restless* 6. *Step by Step* 7. *Chalkzone* 8. *The George Wendt Show* 9. *A Minute with Stan Hooper*

More Publications from Wisconsin Answers: 1. *Airwaves* 2. *Antique Trader* 3. *Arctic Anthropology* 4. *Bead Style* 5. *Big Reel* 6. *Birder's World* 7. *Cheese Reporter* 8. *Country Woman* 9. *Crop Science* 10. *EAA Sport Pilot* 11. *Numismatic News* 12. *Silent Sports* 13. *Taste of Home* 14. *The Harmonizer* 15. *The Progressive* 16. *The Timber Producer* 17. *The Writer* 18. *Trains* 19. *Wisconsin Outdoor Journal* 20. *World Airshow News*

Wisconsin and Space Trivia Answers: 1. Contact 2. Married couple 3. University of Wisconsin-Madison 4. Belleville, Elmwood, Dundee 5. St. John's Northwestern Military Academy 6. Refracting telescope 7. Milwaukee 8. Spaceport 9. Sputnik IV

Wisconsin Astronaut Quote Game Answers: A. Oneida B. French fries C. Envisioned D. Hideout E. Lumber F. Thurston Howell III G. *There's Something about Mary* H. Weapons I. Pavilions J. Faculty K. Waffles L. Catnapped M. Tinsel N. Infinity O. Sweeps P. Casinos Q. Auditory
"The eight years that I spent at the University of Wisconsin-Madison I have incredibly fond memories of. It's a beautiful place with four seasons up in Wisconsin and really wonderful people."

Hollywood Quote Game Answers:
Jackie Mason: A. Mystery B. *Thumbelina* C. Holstein D. Longevity E. Homogeneous
F. Atheism G. Effuse Quote: "I have enough money to last me the rest of my life unless I buy
something."

Chris Farley: A. Latin B. Juvenile C. Physical D. Flycatcher E. Rotary F. Lifeboats G.
Olympians H. Maude Quote: "Basically, I only play one character; I just play him at different
volumes."

Harrison Ford: A. Farmhouse B. Prescription C. Touchy D. Sloth E. Flamenco F. Loretta
G. Admitted H. Ending Quote: "I don't use any particular method. I'm from the let's-pretend
school of acting."

Spencer Tracy: A. Rehearse B. Waddle C. Powerful D. Witnesses E. Conditioner F. Whisked
G. Maintain H. Twosome I. Tahitian J. Myths Quote: "There were times when my pants were
so thin, I could sit on a dime and know if it was heads or tails."

Wisconsin's World Capitals Unscramble Answers: Belleville, Bloomer, Bonduel, Boscobel,
Boulder Junction, Cumberland, Eagle River, Ellsworth, Fremont, Gleason, Glidden, Green Bay,
Mercer, Monroe, Mount Horeb, Norwalk, Onalaska, Oxbo, Park Falls, Presque Isle, Racine,
Somerset, Taycheedah, Warrens, Wausau, Wautoma

Wisconsin's World Capitals Word Find Answers

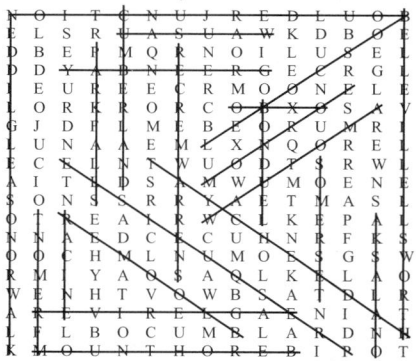

More Wisconsin Waterfalls Answers

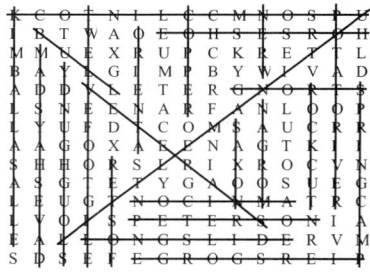

More Wisconsin Lighthouses Answers

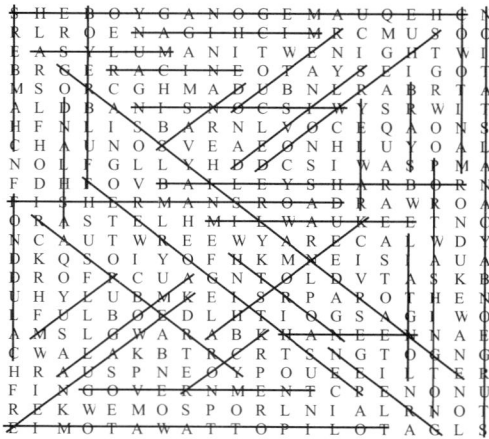